ALLAN KING'S
A MARRIED COUPLE

Long before 'Reality TV,' Canadian filmmaker Allan King caused a stir by
mixing people's private and public lives in his 1969 documentary *A Married Couple*. This observational cinema piece, which took an unscripted
look at the urban Edwards family, was deemed too contentious to air
by commissioning network CTV on the grounds of excessive nudity and
obscenity. Nevertheless, it was accepted by the Cannes festival, and is
now cited as a milestone in realist filmmaking.

In *Allan King's 'A Married Couple,'* Zoë Druick examines the film in the
context of late 1960s cinematic and cultural movements. Through a
scene-by-scene synopsis and an analysis of contemporary responses to
the piece, she traces it's influence on documentary and Canadian filmmaking. The fifth volume in the Canadian Cinema series, this study is
an accessible and engaging introduction to a controversial film and its
fascinating director.

ZOË DRUICK is an associate professor in the School of Communication at
Simon Fraser University.

ALLAN KING'S

A MARRIED COUPLE

ZOË DRUICK

UNIVERSITY OF TORONTO PRESS
Toronto Buffalo London

© University of Toronto Press Incorporated 2010
Toronto Buffalo London
www.utppublishing.com
Printed in Canada

ISBN: 978-1-4426-4245-4 (cloth)
ISBN: 978-1-4426-1133-7 (paper)

Printed on acid-free and 100% post-consumer recycled paper with
vegetable-based inks.

Library and Archives Canada Cataloguing in Publication

Druick, Zoë
    Allan King's A married couple / Zoë Druick.

    (Canadian cinema ; 5)
    Includes bibliographical references.
    ISBN 978-1-4426-4245-4 (bound)   ISBN 978-1-4426-1133-7 (pbk.)

    1. King, Allan, 1930– – Criticism and interpretation.   2. Married
    couple (Motion picture).   I. Title.   II. Title: Married couple.
    III. Series: Canadian cinema (Toronto, Ont.) ; 5.

    PN1997.M365D78 2010   791.4302'33092   C2010-903991-2

TIFF and the University of Toronto Press acknowledge the financial
assistance of the Ontario Media Development Corporation, the Canada
Council for the Arts, and the Ontario Arts Council.

This book has been published with the help of a grant from the Canadian
Federation for the Humanities and Social Sciences, through the Aid to
Scholarly Publications Programme, using funds provided by the Social
Sciences and Humanities Research Council of Canada.

University of Toronto Press acknowledges the financial support of the
Government of Canada through the Canada Book Fund for its publishing
activities.

To Barbara Godard, teacher and friend

Contents

Acknowledgments

I'd like to express my gratitude to Will Straw and Bart Beaty for giving me the opportunity to contribute this volume to the Canadian Cinema series at University of Toronto Press. Siobhan McMenemy, Ryan Van Huijstee, and Frances Mundy efficiently and supportively shepherded the manuscript through the publishing procedure. Thanks to those who read the manuscript along the way and shared their comments, especially Bart Beaty, Sharla Sava, Heidi Schafer, Cheryl Sourkes, Rebecca Sullivan, Will Straw, and two anonymous reviewers for University of Toronto Press. Your generosity and insight were much appreciated. For the unstinting sharing of images, my thanks to Allan King and Amanda Gordon of Allan King Films Ltd. Laurynas Navidauskas provided outstanding research assistance. Above all, my thanks to Billy, Antoinette, and Bogart Edwards for their courageous decision to participate in the making of this film in 1968; and to Allan King, Richard Leiterman, Arla Saare, and their crew for the astounding ability to realize the idea of an 'actuality drama' such as this.

ALLAN KING'S
A MARRIED COUPLE

Introduction

> In *A Married Couple* life is imitating art ... The result may not be entirely candid but it is undeniably real ... Whether it is more or less 'real' than 'real life' is irrelevant; it is a masterful and highly innovative work of art and must be seen.[1]

> If my hunch is correct, what we're seeing in King's new film is not a completely candid and off-guard close-up of an authentic marriage in trouble, as the production purports to be, but to some extent a staged, calculated, louder-than-life 'dramatization' of that marriage produced for public scrutiny.[2]

> In my square world husbands and wives don't fight or make love in public. Allan King's *A Married Couple* does, and if they don't mind exposing their innermost feelings and their most visible weaknesses for all to see, more power to them.[3]

These reactions to Allan King's film *A Married Couple* give some sense of the controversy it excited among filmgoers and critics when it was released in 1969. The film, stemming from King's interest in the tendency of intimacy towards dysfunction, reverberated with wider cultural concerns about candid cameras in the domestic sphere. Made with the Edwards family of Toronto over the summer of 1968, the film challenged ideas about the clear separation between documentary and fiction while highlighting the performative aspect of private life.

Although the idea of recording and exposing ordinary life is arguably a foundational part of the documentary impulse, a corrective to the artificial fantasy of mainstream fiction perhaps, King's version was entirely of its moment. In the late 1960s both traditional domestic and traditional cinematic forms were, in different ways, being brought under scrutiny. King's strategy of using observational documentary to explore the changing experience of the nuclear family was extremely timely. While in many ways *A Married Couple* is an important precursor to the cultural mainstay of reality TV, an adequate examination of the film must imagine it in the context of the emergence and maturation of observational cinema, feminist challenges to post-war conservative visions of the family, and the popularization of post-Freudian therapeutic discourse.

The profound changes in the private sphere demanded the same sort of documentary attention as did issues about public institutions. Yet the revolutionary processes under way in the family exceeded traditional forms. The problem was how to capture these shifts in intimate life on film. The conventions of earlier forms – dramatic and documentary alike – seemed too set, too stilted, to capture the uncertainties of the moment. The dominant documentary idiom was observational, and even drama was being influenced by the sense of immediacy that could be conveyed by spontaneous dialogue in relation to improvised camera-work.

Allan King was of the generation that came of age in the 1950s, and his interest in observational cinema was influenced by both psychotherapy and the Living Theatre. Born in Vancouver in 1930, during the 1960s he lived in Spain and then in London, where early in the 1960s he directed Living Theatre pieces. He settled in Toronto in the mid-1960s and lived there until his death in 2009.[4] He also engaged throughout his life with issues of therapy. He noted, for example, the ability of the camera to spark 'willingness to communicate.' About *A Married Couple*, he said, 'the film is setting [the performers] free in a certain respect ... It isn't just the filming itself which is liberating; it is the creative relationship formed between the subject and myself.'[5] As these quotations indicate, King's emphasis was on filmmaking as process; he said: 'What other people put into scripts and screenplays I put into creating these special relationships, which alone make the film possible.'[6] Reports of King's directorial style emphasize his lack of ego on set. In many cases, as in *A Married Couple*, he often entirely absented himself from the scene of shooting.[7]

This orientation towards experiment and discovery that King tapped into was in many ways quite different from the tradition of public service documentary emblematized by the National Film Board of Canada. King was exploring something beyond rational public communication, though it was arguably no less political.[8] His timing was impeccable. After a decade of observational cinema, by the late 1960s observational filmmakers had begun to turn their cameras from the highly marketable documents of popular youth culture, especially music, to other, more diverse, topics. The cinema of King's contemporary, American filmmaker Frederick Wiseman, beginning in 1967 with *Titicut Follies*, was opening up the ambit of observational cinema to institutional life.[9] As well, Paula Rabinowitz notes the incursion in the late 1960s and early 1970s of observation into formerly private spaces: 'What had begun as the private exposure of public events and figures had inverted into the public display of private, even secret, lives ... The zone of privacy that was family and personal life had become deeply politicised in the late 1960s. Moreover, economic and social factors affecting the middle-class family exploded its 1950s "father knows best" image: rising divorce rates, the demise of the family wage, increasing female labour force participation, open explorations of sexuality.'[10] New forms of documentary were needed to express the social changes under way.

A Married Couple traces the emotional intensity found in the daily life of a couple with a young son. In many ways it is a film that defies categories. It has been called a 'non-fiction feature,' an 'actuality drama,' 'dramatic non-fiction,' and a 'psychodrama.' It resides in the murky hybridities of the docu-fictional. While today a reassessment of textual and ontological distinction between fiction and documentary is under way, King waded into these treacherous waters without a guide. The result is something entirely unique and still hard to define. The secret to its longevity, despite its topical engagements with issues of performance and social experiment, is that it tends more towards the opening up of normative social frameworks than towards the provision of interpretation. Throwing away plot, King offers the viewer an opportunity to share the affective dimensions of a social institution in trouble.

Despite its run-in with censors in Ontario for its swearing and nudity, it went on to a highly respectable theatrical run, both in Canada and abroad. It had an impact on the growing genre of non-fiction drama and was cited, for example, as an inspiration by Craig Gilbert, producer of *An American Family*.[11] Today, in an era of reality-based programming, the importance of the film as a pioneer in mobilizing observational media in personal spaces is inarguable.

Yet, if anything, as time passes, the originality and insight of *A Married Couple* come into even greater focus. The film's contribution to analyses of performance in art and everyday life, for instance, is immeasurable. In 1968 the young British psychoanalyst R.D. Laing delivered the annual Massey Lectures in Toronto. The title of his talks was 'The Politics of the Family'; his theme was the family drama. His ideas give an indication of King's topicality. The 'dramatic structure' of families is, Laing stipulated, 'as a rule, not experienced by, and is unknown to, the very people who generate and perpetuate it ... A scenario is a set of instructions for a play. But these scenarios, if they exist, are unwritten, and, if a part of a scenario sometimes appears in the lines of the play itself, those who enunciate it are usually deeply unaware that they are doing so ... We cannot expect to catch the curtain going up or down in a drama we are born into."[12]

When Laing composed these comments, he was contributing to a resonant discourse within the therapeutic and philosophical communities, one that had achieved a high level of popular acceptance. A decade earlier the sociologist Erving Goffman had introduced the idea of the performance of self to general consciousness with his book *The Presentation of Self in Everyday Life* (1959).[13] This brand of symbolic interactionism propagated the idea of people as social actors who constituted their realities through engagement in socially organized situations, the stages of everyday life. The family, no less than other institutions, was seen as productive of a powerful compulsion to act in ways that might be experienced as oppressive, or inauthentic. By the time Laing gave his lectures, the metaphor of the theatrical in the everyday had achieved a kind of common sense.

Of course, the theatrical metaphor has been an integral part of western thought for centuries. Many everyday conversations are impossible to imagine without theatrical terms such as 'act,' 'action,' 'role,' 'play,' and 'performance.'[14] A persistent site of fascination and desire, theatre has long been associated with the attempt to delude both oneself and others. Certainly, in documentary film studies, the theatrical and the performative pose difficult challenges and at times have stood as the antithesis of the documentary project.[15] Many early film theorists, including Sergei Eisenstein and Dziga Vertov, made strong arguments that film should differentiate itself from theatre absolutely, through emphasis on camera techniques such as montage and close-ups. In this, documentary shares the Enlightenment antipathy to theatre. Yet in the post-war period, theatricality in the everyday took on a new resonance, influenced in part by symbolic interactionism and in part by therapeutic discourses of authentic living.

The epistemological question of the theatrical was taken up and given an affective twist by the notion of the therapeutic theatre found in psychodrama. A product of turn-of-the-century Vienna, psychodrama's founder Joseph Levy Moreno moved to New York State in 1925, where around his method of action therapy, he established a small empire, which he ran with his wife, Zerka Moreno, until his death in 1974. Psychodrama's emphasis on group interaction and 'relationship-based psychotherapy' became a significant influence on the post-war self-help movement.[16] According to this theory, acting out became a way of bringing the unconscious to the surface. Psychodrama cast the analysand as a protagonist working with a 'director' in a spontaneous group drama in which the protagonist's psychic issues could be externalized and confronted. In psychodrama, as in the method acting promulgated by the Actor's Studio, doing became more important than analysing. Both psychodrama and method acting were techniques for externalizing the internal world without the constraints of language. Contrary to the widespread anti-theatrical prejudice, psychodrama made claims for drama's ability to actualize repressed reality.[17]

At the same time as the theatrical was becoming a popular cultural idiom, practitioners of experimental and avant-garde theatre were questioning the conventions of the stage. The sentiment of avant-garde theatre of this period can be encapsulated by the following question: 'How do we know we are watching theatre and not simply observing the world around us?' For many artists experimenting with theatrical practice, the answer was to place emphasis on the frame itself – the stage – as the technology that created spectator and theatrical event alike. Groups such as the Living Theatre – America's best-known avant-garde theatre company – brought these questions to the fore, attempting to stimulate revolutions in perception, which could exert influence outside the theatrical experience.[18] If perceptual patterns reinforced social norms – indeed *were* social norms – then interrupting perception at the artistic level could have an effect on other social regulations. The avant-garde's ideas about the blurring of lines between art and life influenced the 1960s counterculture's loosely associated ideas about be-ins and happenings.

Although not usually thought about in this context, observational cinema emerged in the same period and shared some features with both post-war avant-garde theatrical theory and therapeutic thought.[19] It relied upon the development of lightweight hand-held cameras and tape-recorders that allowed for live, synchronous sound and the capture of uncontrolled, spontaneous situations. Live theatre could be found anywhere. These technical elements were seen not only to comprise one aspect of the film, but rather to be central to its overriding style. Moreover, there was a sense of immediacy in the transformation of event into finished film. With its pans and zooms and overall shaky, hand-held quality, filming tended to draw attention to the film apparatus itself. The sense of 'being there' was an essential part of what lent this kind of filmmaking its feeling of authenticity. Not only was the emphasis on authentic performance, but, as in the theatrical avant-garde, the observational cinema frame was clearly accentuated.

Some observational filmmakers were quite willing to admit that their subjects were 'performing' for the camera; its introduction into a situation was seen as bringing about a heightened self-awareness. For many, the absence of on-camera interviews, additional music, or narration was *de rigueur*. For all practitioners, the truth of the film was linked to its adequacy in representing the filmmaker's experience; hence, it was essential for the filmmaker to be involved in the editing process. Bucking against both the content and the institutional practices of earlier documentary, 1960s observational cinema was not just a form, but also a more or less avant-garde rebellion against traditional filmmaking practices.

Observational cinema techniques may be put to many uses, of course. But the debates in the era of its emergence were conspicuously concerned with achieving authenticity and 'truth' – not guaranteed through these technologies, to be sure, but nonetheless facilitated by them. The technology did not provide an automatic route to veracity, but by using it, filmmakers with a desire to cut through existing documentary conventions, could take a step towards a new ethos. There were different schools. In general, French cinéma-vérité practitioners utilized the camera to provoke engagement, while American direct cinema filmmakers expressed a pronounced scepticism about language, choosing to focus instead on behaviours that could be observed. In an interview in the early 1960s one of the innovators of the American style, journalist Robert Drew, characterized his vision by using the theatrical metaphor: 'It would be a theatre without actors. It would be plays without playwrights. It would be reporting without summary and opinion. It would be the ability to look in on people's lives at crucial times from which you could deduce certain things, and see a kind of proof that can only be gotten through personal experience.'[20] Drew's perspective shares with post-war avant-garde theatre and method acting a general distrust of language as a means of communication. However, it seems significant that along with avant-garde theatre and psychodrama, he too places emphasis on filming the theatre of everyday life.

On the part of some observational filmmakers, and likely film subjects as well, there was a direct engagement with the discourses of therapy. Ever since anthropologist-filmmaker Jean Rouch and sociologist Edgar Morin had encouraged people to talk in the presence of the camera in *Chronique d'une été* (1961), observational cinema had been open to the role of camera as provocateur. What were being captured on film were precisely the kinds of heightened performances the camera could elicit. While American observational filmmaking tended to emphasize public performance, another strain, of which King was a part, focused on the private realm and the need for intimate communication and personal self-reflection. For this strand of filmmaking, truth has a psychoanalytic resonance 'because of the way the camera brings to the surface what is normally hidden or repressed in the subject's social personality.'[21]

This psychological or therapeutic understanding was closely related to the relationship of the filmmaker to film subject. In a sense both were equally exposed and the interaction had to be an ethical one predicated on mutual trust. Michael Chanan sums it up well: 'What observational documentary proposed is difficult, perhaps impossible, and depends on both the filmmaker's competence and the subject's assent and co-operation. The subject must feel the filmmaker can be trusted and the documentarist must work to create conditions of acceptance.'[22] The desire and ability to foreground the role of the filmmaker in facilitating and provoking the filmed encounter is quite unique to observational documentary.

A Married Couple emerged from this period of exploration and questioning and in some ways is its most accomplished experiment. The film, its context, and its reception can give us insight into the workings of culture and the importance of aesthetic texts for crystallizing social issues and inspiring debate. With this study of *A Married Couple*, I hope to bring to light the ways in which a historical text may provide insight not only about the time in which it was made, but also about issues that have emerged in its wake. Reality-based media are now central in mainstream culture, but their texts, not to mention the terms in which they are popularly discussed, are rarely revealing. I propose that their analysis might be enriched by attention to historical predecessors such as *A Married Couple*.

For instance, today, the preponderance of reality-based programming on television has made aspects of the idea of everyday performance commonplace. The fact of ordinary people performing for the camera has become an increasingly familiar feature of both amateur media usage and large-scale entertainment. The question of authenticity is routinely invoked. Yet the social analysis mobilized by 1960s practitioners and theorists of observation, performance, and theatricality is often lost. Too often in public discourse truth is conflated with the technological means of reproduction. The avant-garde idea of using media experimentation to challenge social norms and frameworks of perception is missing. The therapeutic idea about evoking truth in performance through relations of trust is nowhere to be found. If anything, today's reality television naturalizes rather than questions the Social Darwinism of competitive capitalism and the governmentalized social context of neoliberalism that it exposes.[23]

In the next chapter, I trace the emergence of the concept behind *A Married Couple* and situate it within the 'dramaturgical perspective' that proliferated in public discourse in the 1960s. In chapter 3, I analyse the film with particular attention to its fraught relationship to the tradition of family melodrama. I postulate that it has much to tell us about its historical context, both social and cinematic, as well as about the dynamism of genre. Critical response to the film is the subject of chapter 4. I propose that Vivian Sobchack's phenomological study of documentary reception is an important clue to the mixed responses the film provoked. The subject of chapter 5 is the significance of the film for current discussions about reality-based media and documentary ethics. I put forward a framework that considers media texts as moments of critique, rather than windows on reality, and postulate that *A Married Couple* is a prime example of 'popular modernism,' a promise inherent in film to reflect our fragmented experiences of everyday life. In conclusion, in chapter 6, I consider the legacy of the film for Canadian cinema and media culture more generally.

On numerous occasions, Allan King disclosed that his formative experience of family disintegration during early childhood in the Depression influenced his lifelong filmic preoccupations. In particular, his father's flight from the family home led him to attempt to understand the element of individual choice in difficult social conditions. The tenuous bonds of intimacy are also a constant refrain in his work. While conceptualizing and making *A Married Couple*, he was going through a divorce from his first wife, Phyllis Leiterman (sister of his collaborators, Richard and Douglas Leiterman). Given these dual affective zones, there is more than an implication that King experienced the Edwards family of the film from two perspectives simultaneously: as adult artist and as bewildered child. As someone born in the month of the film's release (November 1969) who also observed as a preschooler the breakdown of my parents' marriage, I think part of the film's lasting appeal is precisely this multi-perspectivalism. The film presents a sort of cubist version of events where no one perspective prevails. King's open-ended philosophy of documentary as a process of discovery for filmmaker, performer, and spectator allows for multiple readings and points of entry. *A Married Couple* is at once a time capsule from the late 1960s and a lasting engagement with the question of intimacy and subjectivity.

Observational Feature Filmmaking
and the 'Dramaturgical Perspective'

In 1967 Allan King, a thirty-seven-year-old Canadian filmmaker with more than a decade of filmmaking experience, released *Warrendale*, a study of a halfway house for emotionally disturbed children and adolescents in North Toronto.[1] King resisted all narration in the film, leaving viewers to decide for themselves what they thought about the therapeutic methods employed with the children, especially a technique of restraint used to placate them when they were agitated. The result is an exceptionally powerful film and, despite being banned by commissioning network, CBC, *Warrendale* attained a number of honours, among them the Prix Art et Essai at Cannes.

After the success of *Warrendale* King had many options for his next film. Dealing at the time with his own marital difficulties as well as memories of his parents' tumultuous relationship, he chose to make a film about marriage; the result was *A Married Couple*, originally intended to be broadcast on CTV. As King has said, 'I thought it would be fascinating and illuminating to stay with the couple and observe ... Most particularly, I was concerned with a marriage in crisis and wanted to observe the kinds of ways in which a couple misperceive each other and carry into the relationship anxieties, childhood patterns, all the things that make up one's own personality and character. But these inevitably distort the other person and make true intimacy or true connection difficult ... It puzzled me that people always seemed to get less from marriage than they wanted.' While raising money for the film, he carried out an extensive search for participants, eventually settling on acquaintances of his, Antoinette and Billy Edwards, an attractive couple with a son, Bogart, aged two and a half years, a dog, Merton, and a seemingly ideal home on a tree-lined street in a 'gentrifying' Toronto neighbourhood west of Bathurst Street near St Clair Avenue. They were paid union-rate hourly wages for the duration of the shoot, which to-talled about $5,000, plus a small percentage of the film's profits.[2]

Here is how *A Married Couple* was shot. First, they worked out how to light the Edwards's home unobtrusively and made a few adjustments to the space, such as covering the dark wood panelling in the living room with burlap. King and his crew showed up early each morning to capture the family waking up and having breakfast, and, after Billy left for work, they would occasionally spend a little more time with either Billy at work or Antoinette and their son Bogart at home before taking a few hours off. The crew returned in time for dinner and the bedtime routine. Cinematographer and associate director Richard Leiterman re-called, 'We never missed a dinner or evening meal. The events of the day would be gone over, and you'd get the scene.' On weekends they arrived at 5 p.m. on Friday and stayed until Sunday evening, grabbing naps when they could. When the family went on a pre-planned vaca-tion to Maine and Vermont, an extra lighting man went on ahead to set up the locations.[3]

After the first three weeks, King decided not to hang around the shoot and instead focused on watching the rushes. Perhaps coinciden-tally, Leiterman noted that the couple became more relaxed during the third week: 'They just seemed to slow down, things weren't so rushed or nervous, and they didn't make so much noise. Maybe they weren't quite so funny when there was no need for it.' In the tenth and final week of shooting the Edwardses had a violent fight followed by an emo-

Allan King around the time of making *A Married Couple*. Courtesy Allan King Films Ltd.

Richard Leiterman. Courtesy Allan King Films Ltd.

Allan King and Richard Leiterman. Courtesy Allan King Films Ltd.

Chris Wangler, sound. Courtesy Allan King Films Ltd.

tional reconciliation, and King felt he had enough material to edit the film.[4]

In the simplest terms, *A Married Couple* observes the relationship of a white, middle-class couple in mid-life (he is forty and she is thirty) with a young family. They wrestle with their intimacy and simultaneously with social gender roles in the nuclear family. Billy works in advertising; Antoinette works in the home. In place of plot, the film offers a compelling series of set pieces in which repetitious emotional scripts are enacted. Although the couple seems unhappy with the marriage most of the time, and many of the scenes are of fighting, they also seem ill equipped to resolve their difficulties. Put differently, the viewer is invited to see that awareness and even insight about problems do not necessarily lead to change, a paradox that was one of the spurs to King's creative vision.[5]

When the Edwardses agreed to participate, their marriage was functioning smoothly. Knowing that King was interested in exploring a marriage in 'crisis ... or conflict,' Billy told King, 'Our marriage isn't that much of a crisis [*sic*] at the moment, so you would have to make a film simply about an everyday marriage.' But King, made aware of undercurrents through the process of his own divorce, sensed that conflicts were there and would arise during shooting.[6] Conflicts did indeed emerge, sparked in part by the presence of the camera, and, although the Edwardses stayed together long enough to have a second child, their marriage, like many in the 1970s, eventually did end in divorce a few years later (1971).

A Married Couple was even more critically successful than *Warrendale*. As Alan Rosenthal wrote soon after the film's release, compared with *Warrendale*, *A Married Couple* seemed 'to be far more innovative in showing future possibilities in direct cinema. What one sees is neither documentary nor fiction drama, but a curious blend of the two formed by creating fictitious emotional links in the editing of documentary footage. [*A Married Couple*] shows a much deeper and more personal concern on the part of the filmmaker for his subject than is seen or felt in most other *vérité* films ... Possibly his talent lies in conceptualizing, organizing, directing, and a certain flair in guiding the editing.'[7] Indeed, Rosenthal predicted that given the film's complex negotiation of fiction and documentary *A Married Couple* would become extremely influential. Like all films about institutions, in this case marriage, the power of the observational style lay in showing the difference between ideology and actuality. As Seth Feldman has put it, the film illustrates the existential axiom: 'life is not what we say it is but how we live it.'[8] In this way, the study of changing social norms dovetailed with the oldest advice in the dramatic lesson book: 'do, don't tell.'

Antoinette and Billy are shown to be struggling and flawed. But *A Married Couple* is a mature film that demands that the viewer not judge the characters, but rather reflect on his or her own relationships and ability to communicate. King emphasized the need to watch empathetically: 'I do maintain that to know all the facts about a person's life tends to suspend judgment. My approach to film is the opposite of the formation of prejudice. A prejudice is established by knowing a few facts and striking an attitude that is essentially inconsistent with those facts. I think a film can unravel people's prejudices. The trick is getting them to consider going to a film that deals with a subject they normally push from their minds. Once they are in the theatre, or auditorium, the film can work on them; the obstacle is getting them there in the first place.'[9] In a sense, this kind of reflection could be provoked only by such an 'actuality drama.' It is precisely because we reflect on their reality as a couple conveyed through the unscripted encounters that demonstrate their charms and flaws for all to see that we are forced to think about the complexity of all relationships. In a fictional piece, the viewer could more easily dismiss even emotionally truthful scenes by chalking them up to dramatic convention.

The exploration King expects from his audience is not unlike his personal one. He related to Bruce Martin a year after the film was completed: 'For me, [making a film] is a process of discovering and expressing what I feel; since I'm very often devious with my own feelings to myself and perhaps to others, it takes an awfully long time for me to really feel and then to get in order and shape whatever I feel. In a lot of ways this is what I've used film for. The marriage film has very much to do with finding out what marriage is about, what is involved in two people's living together: what's that like, what do I feel about it, what goes astray, how do people miss, how are they good with each other ... Once it's finished it becomes a closed book.'[10]

King was always exceedingly clear about the film's fictions. For example, seventy hours of footage shot over ten weeks was edited down to just over ninety-six minutes, an astronomical shooting ratio of 44:1. Even those seventy hours represent but a fragment of the eight years Billy and Antoinette had spent together by the time the film was shot in the summer of 1968. Rather than see the film as a transparent window onto the Edwards's relationship, King astutely labelled the film more generically as about a particular kind of relationship – marriage – and frankly acknowledged the effect of both camera and editor on the everyday performances filmed. As King put it, 'One has to be very, very clear. Billy and Antoinette in the film are not Billy and Antoinette Edwards, the couple who exist and live at 323 Rushton Road. They are characters, images on celluloid in a film drama. To say that they are in any other sense true, other than being true to our experience of the world and people we have known and ourselves, is philosophical nonsense. There is no way ninety minutes in a film of Billy and Antoinette can be the same as the actual real life of Billy and Antoinette.'[11]

King called the work an 'actuality drama.' The film's veteran editor, Arla Saare, called it 'a fiction documentary.' These terms are redolent of Frederick Wiseman's labels of his own work as 'reality dreams' and 'reality fictions.'[12] In both cases, the filmmakers refuse the chrono-logic of many observational films and instead boldly subordinate the material to their own vision of the truth of events.[13] Thus, instead of following events in the order in which they occurred, the events are allowed to take on a more generalized character and a more conceptual editing structure. For example, rather than a scene depicting breakfast on 12 July 1968 with a subtitle notifying viewers of the date, it is simply 'breakfast,' part of the repetitive, trivial, and mundane routines out of which life is crafted. A few years later, Craig Gilbert would make the same discoveries in *An American Family*. As Jeffrey Ruoff notes about that production, 'the emphasis of the observational style on singular events was mitigated by the repetitiveness of everyday life.'[14]

In both films, the editors crafted these many observed details into a narrative with seemingly causal relationships. Saare and King started by cutting into sequences all the material they deemed interesting– 'a great deal of the film was very boring,' Saare acknowledged. These sequences they assembled into a general structure. '*A Married Couple* was so different,' Saare observed, 'because it needed the director and myself to talk constantly about the impact of the scenes, to discuss structure, to cut it down where we felt either one was being maligned or not being fair to another person. It was much more a twosome in this marriage film than any other film I had worked on.'[15]

The end result represents a compromise between fidelity to the actual situation and the conventions of viewing. For example, in *A Married Couple*, a sequence in which Antoinette is seen flirting with someone at a party is followed by a scene in which she is extremely upset and crying. The film allows us to think that the flirting at the party led to a situation in which the strains in Billy and Antoinette's relationship were beginning to become permanent rifts. However, both the party scene (actually organized for the film) and the crying scene (apparently related to intense emotions brought on by the end of the film shoot)

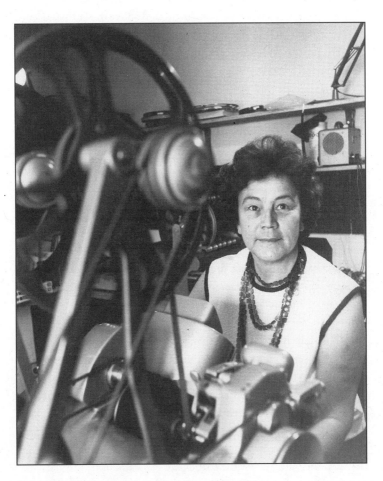

Arla Saare, editor. Courtesy Allan King Films Ltd.

were brought together in a way that, though not causally related, well expressed the issues of marital strife being explored by King. Although these tensions were heightened by the making of the film, the underlying emotions were real and intrinsic to the Edwards's marriage. As King has responded when people have asked about the authenticity of certain scenes, '"Is it really real"? – what the hell does that mean? Either the film means something to you, or it doesn't.'[16] In other words, it bears remembering that at the end of the day what we have is a *film*, not two new friends. However, despite King's reticence to categorize the film (as we will see in chapter 4), responses to the film hinged precisely on viewer expectation. Genre would not be willed away.

Associative dream logic is an element at play in *A Married Couple* as much as in the films of Wiseman. For Wiseman, the emphasis is on the non-logical associations that he makes with the material in the editing room; for King, the issue concerns the performance of self for the camera. In an interview he explained, 'And there is another question some people raise: Are they acting? And it sort of begs the question, because even if they were acting, where did the stuff come from? You know, it's like dreams. They are your dreams. The action in the dream is yours because you have remembered the dream and you have created the dream. And the feelings are what you may act with or pretend with. So they are valid. Feelings in a sense are unchallenged. Unchallengeable. But they are often surprising.'[17] In other words, performing the self for the camera, not unlike recalling dreams, is a way to make the unconscious conscious. However, 'playing out' feelings and becoming aware of the emotional foundation of action doesn't necessarily lead to mastery and closure. In the method subscribed to by King at this point in his career, the process was a way of creating an authentic film text. In this way it differs in intention and result from a therapeutic practice in which the outcome for the participant is paramount.

Still, using real people as performers raises its own set of issues and excites certain questions about the effect of the filming. Wiseman has argued that when faced with a camera in a public setting, people will behave normally, if not naturally: 'I think the great subject of documentary is normalcy or what passes for normal behaviour.'[18] In the private sphere, things may not work exactly this way. While the couple often behaves 'normally' in the film when in public, at work, out with friends, or on the phone, at home they are also living through an experiment that is questioning norms. Countercultural ideas and behaviours have seeped into what in many ways is otherwise a conventional middle-class life, rendering everything uncertain. Billy, who appears in much of the film wearing little more than red bikini briefs, apparently would not have worn any underwear were he not asked to do so by King.

'The first week we were shooting,' recalled Leiterman, 'we were there for morning wakeup and Billy got out of bed and tramped around the house, went down and called the dog, and then went out in the backyard and played with the dog – all this completely naked. We felt that maybe that particular thing was set up for us – maybe he was doing it for our benefit – but it was just Billy acting normally.'[19] Yet, despite this casual approach to clothing, he can be seen at numerous times in the film smoking a pipe and ruminating about the respect owing to him as the man of the house. Being nude at home may be nothing more than a revised version of 'my home is my castle,' but it simultaneously seems to shed the bourgeois conventions of respectability and propriety. So either the nudity reflects a new version of propriety – it is more authentic to be completely comfortable, clothing makes me uncomfortable – or it is a complex and possibly contradictory aspect of the Edwards's lives, poised as they are between social convention and individual self-realization.

As Leiterman noted at the time, 'The presence of the camera tends to distort at the beginning of any real filming. People are trying their best to be normal people; but in doing so, I would think that the majority of them find they are acting.'[20] To get a better sense of what he might have meant by this, I turn to Erving Goffman's well-known study of everyday human behaviour, *The Presentation of Self in Everyday Life.* Goffman postulates that everyday life is made up of a series of performances that constitute our personae. The performers need to believe in their 'roles' and convince others of their sincerity. The performance takes place on certain 'sets' and the roles we adopt become 'fact.' His 'dramaturgical perspective' can be summed up with his phrase: 'Life itself is a dramatically enacted thing.'[21]

According to Goffman's analysis, ordinary social discourse is put together in the way a theatrical scene might be. So, for example, there is a difference between front- and backstage behaviours, costumes, and scripts, and between sets of discursive possibilities. Those with whom we are intimately engaged may see us backstage, but most others may only see us in the 'front' regions of our lives. Others, whom he terms 'outsiders,' may not see us at all. In a society where our lives largely play out indoors, outsiders are people who are not allowed into our private spaces. In his words: 'Performers appear in the front and back regions; the audience appears only in the front region; and the outsiders are excluded from both regions.'[22] Goffman's schema of everyday performance gives us some insight into the radical project of *A Married Couple*. The filmmakers' presence with the family backstage in bedrooms and bathrooms transgresses the normal line of demarcation between audience and performer.

In the couple's bathroom, a picture of Pierre Elliott Trudeau is conspicuously taped to the wall, presumably ripped from a magazine. It shows the then prime minister baring his teeth in his inscrutable smile. No doubt the image is there to underscore the film's ironic comment on Trudeau's 1967 assertion that 'there's no place for the state in the bedrooms of the nation.' The state may be exiled, but the public will not be kept out. As in other observational films about performers from the 1960s, such as Jane Fonda in *Jane* (1962), or Bob Dylan in *Dont Look Back* (1967), the performance in backstage regions becomes the index of the film's authenticity. However, because what we see 'backstage' in *A Married Couple* is the private life of otherwise ordinary individuals, the transgression is keenly felt by viewers.

Because of its off-limits status, personal and domestic space holds a tantalizing mystery. Partly this fascination has been used to explain the popularity of webcams and certain reality TV shows such as *Big Brother* and *Real World*. But contest-based reality TV shows, such as *Survivor* and *Canada's Next Top Model*, also capitalize on this desire by building an aspect of performed intimacy into their format in the guise of the confessional. Often filmed in a special 'offstage' space, the confessional segments are supposed to give the viewer a special intimacy with contestants, hearing the things they will say when none of the other contestants is around.

However, in *A Married Couple* not only are the filmmakers themselves present backstage, but they are making a recording that opens up the participants' lives for all to see, including complete strangers. In so doing, the filmmakers bring the audience associated with – and even required by – the front-stage activities to backstage life, where it is supposedly anathema. The result is a complex performance that brings to the fore the regulated aspects of private life, including its need for a backstage. Yet, as we are invited to see, the backstage is no less dramaturgical; its dramaturgy is simply of a different kind. In Goffman's analysis, the backstage is not unlike the unconscious part of subjectivity, where formalities vanish and 'the suppressed facts make an appearance.'[23] *A Married Couple* shows us the cultural aspect of the unconscious.

According to Michael Chanan, *A Married Couple* and *An American Family* are 'living room' films with a voyeuristic promise of 'crossing boundaries and witnessing the intimate.' 'The private house, where people do control their own space, is shut off from public access, a place where guests and strangers (including the camera) enter only by invitation, and are then usually restricted to certain rooms, where in other words certain rooms are more private than others.'[24] The films offer a promise of entering a backstage zone, going behind the scenes into a semi-private space. But what we find in the private realm is the engagement of self with social desires and frameworks, the anxieties of a striving middle class in search of 'self and status.'[25] Indeed, there are few surprises when the lid is pried off the home. Although the everyday contradictions of front- and backstage take on a heightened form when brought together in film, the result seems closer to an illustration of Slavoj Žižek's reading of the unconscious than to Goffman's. Far from the private realm being a spatial signifier for the relaxation of regulation, in the inner reaches of the home we see the backstage as the ego's strongest governor.[26]

The film does not show us something we are unaware of: the conflicts and dysfunctionalities of intimacy at the heart of marriage have been experienced or witnessed by virtually everyone. But all the same, the individual ways in which the couple grapples with larger social structures are revealing. In acting out with spontaneous dramaturgy their own private drama, their story takes on the powerful resonance of all good drama.

A Married Couple uses its performative premise to explore authenticity and self-actualization. In this, it is of its moment. The late 1960s constituted a period dominated by concerns about liberation, both political and personal. New social movements and new artistic movements converged. and both the politics of art and the aesthetics of everyday life drew heightened attention. A shift in sexual relations was under way, although its politics was unclear. Did the birth control pill liberate women or re-subordinate them to the sexual demands of patriarchy?

By the end of the 1960s this movement had gone mainstream and had even become self-parodic. How else to explain the numerous awards bestowed on Paul Mazursky's comedy *Bob & Carol & Ted & Alice* (1969) for its screenplay about upper-class California couples experimenting with gestalt therapy and sexual swinging? The 1969 musical *Hair* sang about the dawning of the Age of Aquarius, an astrological explanation for the change in social values that was widely discussed in terms of a new age. (Reflecting these ideas, Allan King's production company for the film was called Aquarius Films.)

The sexual politics of the era made the home a political site. The technologized new woman of the 1920s was reinvigorated by the relaxing of post-war conservatism, and men of the era were 'in danger of losing their strategic dominance.'[27] What could make a better subject for a film about families than sexual politics? Just as documentaries of the 1930s had concentrated on the major political upheavals of that era, late 1960s and early 1970s documentary took up the pressing question of the modern family. According to Paula Rabinowitz: 'once the organization of personal life became a legitimate focus of political activism, it also became a significant site for the *vérité* camera as well ... The living room was as likely as the boardroom – more so actually if you believed in women's liberation calls to make the personal political – to reveal the contradictions of American capitalism. History unfolded in the crevices of the home as much as it did on the streets or in the courts, statehouses, corporations, and factory floors.'[28]

The truly observational film cannot give access to what is going on inside the actors' heads, as can happen in a realist novel. Sarah Kozloff argues that the act of 'overhearing' is central to the experience of dramatic cinema, where supposedly private encounters are routinely offered to us. Viewers, she writes, 'are eavesdroppers, listening in on conversations that – in reality – are designed to communicate certain information to the audience.' This demands certain features of dramatic dialogue, what Kozloff calls a 'double-layeredness.' For instance, words are 'directed at the filmgoer, not at the on-screen conversationalists,'[29] but must sound natural all the same. However, in an unscripted shooting situation the issue is brought to a head. The dialogue becomes the most important means of conveying characters' feelings and gathering information to contextualize action, yet the primary goal of the actors is not necessarily to make their motives transparent. The filmmaker must focus equally on detail and on spaces of performance. Michael Chanan proposes that observational cinema highlights the performance of the subject in particular spaces, or what he usefully calls 'revelation through situation.'[30]

For this reason, Bill Nichols has aptly called observational cinema

a vivid form of 'present-tense' representation ... For the viewer, observational documentaries set up a frame of reference closely akin to that of fiction film ... We look in on and overhear social actors ... The performance of social actors ... is similar to the performance of fictional characters in many respects. Individuals present a more or less complex psychology, and we direct our attention toward their development or destiny. We identify and follow the codes of actions and enigmas that advance the narrative. We attend to those semic or behaviourally descriptive moments that fold back over characters and give further density to their behaviour. We give considerable attention to the referential codes imported or 'documented' by the text as the operational codes of the culture that the social actors adhere to or contest in discernible ways.[31]

More even than with fictional characters, in documentary viewers may consider the characters' surroundings, not to mention their costumes and the choice of music as clues of self-expression. All are expressions of subjectivity to the eyes of the world. Facial expression and action become equally important modes for determining characters' inner conflicts. Close-ups take on an added significance in our attempt to read characters' emotions through their faces. In an improvised situation, the cameraman has to anticipate the emotional core of each scene and find revealing images for its expression.

By using 'real' people willing to explore the nature of the married state, King was able to bring to the surface this complex of issues about 'the dramaturgical perspective.' Despite the film's undeniably documentary aspect, it also became, through *mise en scène* and editing, an extremely well-crafted narrative. As Arla Saare put it: 'At the end of the film I know that under my hand we had isolated segments out of two people's lives, in a rather cohesive order; and it showed Billy and Antoinette in a very sympathetic light. I think the film has charm, humour, violence, and that they are two very ordinary, very wonderful people.'[32]

A Married Couple as Documentary Melodrama

From its opening credits, *A Married Couple* signals both its authenticity and its ambiguity. Without narration or explanatory text, the credits both claim the subject's 'reality' and refuse to label the finished product as either documentary or fiction, calling it simply 'a film':

> *A Married Couple*
> *Billy and Antoinette Edwards*
> *Their child Bogart*
> *Their dog Merton*
> *In a film by Allan King*

The fact of real people as actors is presented simultaneously with the authorial stamp of the filmmaker. The phrase 'a married couple' thus takes on a descriptive aspect regarding the Edwardses and at the same time becomes the abstract or generic title of the film made with and about them. The light-hearted guitar music used throughout cues the listener to expect something entertaining rather than educational.

Although mainly filmed in the home, there are a number of significant secondary locations, including a rural vacation landscape, Billy's workplace, and Antoinette's outside activities. (For a chronology of scenes see figure 6.) Despite primary reliance on an observational style, there are five crane shots in the film, giving a wider social perspective to the hothouse of the domestic sphere. For instance, the film begins with a night-time crane shot of the Edwards house, providing the sense of omniscience we are used to in fiction films. The use of crane shots or extreme long shots as transitions between episodes, at the beginning of the film in particular, renders the story more allegorical and clearly foregrounds the artifice of the filming, such shots being the antithesis of spontaneous filmmaking. The crane shots that position the characters in the social world occur early in the story: the house at night and in the morning, Billy going to work, and Antoinette at a café with a friend. However, as the film progresses, the camera increasingly traps the viewer, like the characters, in the claustrophobia and conflict of the domestic context.

In the first sequence of the film we are introduced to the camera's ability to permeate the fourth wall of the domestic theatre. In a high crane shot we see and hear people leaving a house on a leafy street, a convention of narrative seen not many years before in the film version of *Who's Afraid of Virginia Woolf?* (1966). With this establishing shot we enter *in medias res* the lives of a couple as they close the door on their departing guests with a playful 'thank God they're gone.' The film immediately welcomes us into the living room, which in this case is a location 'behind the scenes' for outsiders. The guests have left, but we, the viewers, are just arriving. The two people reveal through their dialogue that they are the married couple of the title, and they embark on two amusing light-hearted routines that will prove paradigmatic for their encounters throughout the film. As he strips down to his underwear, Billy regales Antoinette somewhat nonsensically about his inability to find comfortable shoes. Antoinette speaks about her decision to buy a harpsichord, setting Billy off about her selfish and unreasonable desires. They also discuss a myriad of material possessions: their new rug and couch, a broken vacuum cleaner, a lamp, and the possibility of buying

Table 3.1   Scene List, A Married Couple

Scene #	Description of scene	length
1	Credit sequence; outdoor crane shot, nighttime; guitar theme	0:00–1:09
2	Living room, bantering fight about harpsichord	1:10–6:08
3	Getting ready for bed; negotiating space in bed	6:09–9:11
4	Outdoor crane shot, morning; waking up; breakfast	9:12–14:48
5	Guitar music; arrival at work in car; crane shot, The Esplanade	14:49–15:29
6	Crane shot on Bloor St.; Antoinette in café with friend	15:30–19:10
7	Billy and Bogart play 'horsey' in the living room; car insurance	19:11–20:12
8	Kitchen renovation discussion over take out dinner in the dining room; discussion of records	20:13–26:20
9	Using the record player	26:21–28:50
10	Dancing in living room	28:51–30:18
11	Discussion in Antoinette's room about fame; 2nd bedroom scene; fight about separate bedrooms	30:19–34:10
12	Antoinette's movement class	34:11–34:39
13	Billy on the phone at work; reads Milt Dunnell text	34:40–36:22
14	Family dinner in the dining room; argument about car, dog food, grand piano	36:23–52:29
15	Billy goes to work; crane shot outside building; Antoinette cleans house	52:30–53:55
16	Family dinner in the dining room; discussion of 'spiritual lux'	53:56–56:26
17	Arrival at cottage in Vermont; lake bathing scene	56:27–61:21
18	Party at a friend's house in Maine; flirting scene	61:22–66:52
19	In diesen heil'gen Hallen embrace	66:53–69:04
20	Waking up in different beds	69:05–69:45
21	Big fight scene culminating in physical violence	69:46–75:46
22	Bogart and Billy watching TV	75:47–76:16
23	Family dinner in dining room; Bogart shits on floor	76:17–82:21
24	Lying in bed discussing relationship; discussion continues in living room; end credits; guitar theme	82:22–96:24

a washer and dryer. Although we immediately take to them as charismatic and engaging people – both had backgrounds in amateur theatre – their conversation is limited to negotiation and consumption. This scene feels very self-consciously played for the camera, and the brightly lit room has the stagey feel of a film set. From the beginning, King highlights the artifice of realism and the struggles to find authenticity on screen. Also, however, the possibility of happiness in consumer culture is clearly thematized.

The bantering fight is followed by the first of four bedroom scenes. Here in the inner sanctum of the married relationship, we are exposed to awkwardness and discomfort – of both the marriage and its public exposure. Leiterman utilizes mirror reflections in his filming of the scene, a traditional motif in melodrama that well expresses the plight of people trapped in inward-looking and stultifying domestic experiences. Their playful violence in this first bedroom scene is repeated later by real violence. So, as in the therapeutic method of psychodrama, even the staginess of the scene does not diminish the reality of the emotions being 'played' out.

The theme of happiness is registered by three uses of the word *joy* in the second and third scenes. The word appears as a brand name in the magazine Antoinette is reading during the bedroom scene. 'Joy' is prominent on the cover of the cookbook she is using during the tense breakfast scene that follows. And when Billy and Antoinette talk to Bogart about crying, they blame his caregiver, Joy, for telling Bogart that 'only babies cry.' Given the tense encounters of these scenes, the repetition of the motif of 'joy' seems highly ironic. In two of the cases, joy has been commodified, stressing its compensatory nature for something lacking from everyday life.

Throughout the film, numerous arguments are enacted about the management of the domestic space. In scene 8, the couple discusses renovating the kitchen. Antoinette's vision of it is dramatic and expansive: Moorish arches, an oven for roasting a whole lamb. Billy points out how unrealistic these fantasies are. Then, as her vision becomes more elaborate, he explodes about 'goddamn faggot-approved' design. While they have this discussion about kitchen renovations, they eat take-out Chinese food from cardboard containers, an irony that leaves the viewer to reflect that the kitchen is more about fashion and the display of wealth and status than it is about practical use. The connection of their relationship to consumption, as well as their mutual discontent, is made clear.

One of the particular features of post-war domestic life is the emergence and proliferation of a series of domestic consumer technologies. The reconfiguring of society into self-contained nuclear family units increasingly came to rely on a range of technologies designed to support both privacy and mobility.[1] *A Married Couple* features numerous scenes in which domestic appliances for cooking, entertainment, and communication become major illustrations of the technologized family home. In one of the central scenes of the film (scene 8), the couple discusses records for their new stereo. Music, a possible indicator of subjectivity, becomes just another agency for culturally produced desires. Dressed in pearls, slip, and black brassiere, Antoinette begins her choices with a classical music shopping list that includes Beethoven's Symphony no. 7, Vivaldi's Four Seasons, and something by that 'mad Russian' Rachmaninoff. She moves on to pop music: 'Alice's Restaurant,' Country Joe and the Fish, and Frank Sinatra. Each composer, piece, or performer is a signifier for, by turns, cultural distinction and youth culture.

A long sequence focused on the record player (scenes 9 and 10) encapsulates the promise and disappointment of consumer society. In close-up we see Billy placing a record on their new player. A zoom-out reveals Bogart and Antoinette sitting nearby, playing. It is a scene of familial intimacy. Antoinette requests the end of the fourth track. The Beatles' *Sgt. Pepper's Lonely Hearts Club Band* blasts out, a huge hit in 1967.

Antoinette looks excited until the record slips. The two sit placidly on the floor with the dog and the baby discussing the problem. Antoinette insists that there is nothing wrong with the stereo; rather, they (meaning Billy) do not know how to use it properly. The arm swings back onto the record, making a loud scratching noise. Here, not only does the music comment on action in ways conventional to melodrama, but the technological medium of the record player adds a dimension of gendered interface. As the scene progresses we see them dancing, framed by the cut-glass panels of the living room door frame. This remarkable shot reiterates the feeling that the living room is a site of intimacy. The camera hovers outside, highlighting the feeling of self-conscious spectatorship. Antoinette grins while Billy carries her, her legs around his waist, in a mock waltz. There is a jumpcut, but the music continues into the breakdown section of the song ('I'd Love to Turn You On'). They do a theatrical dance together, having moved well beyond the conventions of waltzing.

Two other technologies figure prominently as key areas of emotional condensation in the film: the car and the vacuum cleaner. Having access to the car provides much needed mobility for Antoinette, but, according to the terms of their relationship, the only way for her to have unrestricted access to it is to drop Billy at work in the morning. The car and its insurance provide a number of moments through which the relationship's tension is staged. Another of the repeated motifs of the film concerns a vacuum cleaner they have recently acquired. The vacuum is supposed to facilitate Antoinette's work in the home but, as with many technologies, it also begins to stand in for the user. When they first buy it Billy asks: 'Did you like it?' Antoinette replies: 'Yes, I did,' wryly adding, 'as much as anyone can like a vacuum cleaner.' But later, during a fight, he refers to her as having a 'vacuumatic little body.'

The scene that features the most intense violence (21) begins with Antoinette, wearing a white minidress with wide lace sleeves and an apron, vacuuming under the dining room table. Billy enters the scene in an orange jumpsuit and says something inaudible, to which Antoinette responds negatively and turns off the vacuum. He is criticizing her use of the appliance. She yells at him and he calls her a 'stupid cunt.' Next, they argue about music again, this time in relation to returning some records to friends. The fight escalates until he physically grabs her by head and neck and wrestles her out the door. She harmlessly flings a beach ball at him, which he ducks as it comes at the camera. He throws some pans at her and slams the door. Opening the door again, he orders her to 'take that stuff and get out.' She warns him 'not to touch' her as he walks back in. We hear him say, 'I'll break your fucking hand.' Framed by the glass panels next to the door we see her walk quickly down the steps. The viewer is trapped inside the domestic enclosure with an angry and abusive Billy.

Television, the most iconic domestic technology of all, appears in the subsequent scene. Antoinette has left and Billy and Bogart watch TV together. Billy is subdued, almost without affect, tapping his hand to some music emanating from the television. We can hear a CBC commentator's voice as the two engage in the lonesome togetherness of television watching. Given the proximity of this scene to the violent fight, we may also wonder about Bogart's exposure to his parents' discord. Is the television offering him something different from what goes on at home?

The acquisition of and relation to consumer technologies is a clear theme throughout the film. In addition, as Billy works in advertising, the film raises the issue of the couple's own self-commodification. In one scene Billy is at work talking on the phone about his ad copy. The ad is apparently a promotional spot for sports journalist Milt Dunnell. 'Anyone can watch,' Billy says. 'It means getting them to open up to him after the action. It's called absolute truth. And he gets it. How does he do it? That's his workaday secret.' Earlier, while Billy was shaving, we heard a Western Union ad: 'Got to get a message to you, Western Union Style.' In similar fashion, Billy's ad thoroughly links communication and consumption. The ad also makes an ironic commentary on observational cinema. Unlike the sports writer in question, King is not trying to get people to open up to him 'after the action.' Rather, he is trying to capture them in action. However, neither this nor the other approach can actually promise 'absolute truth.' Contrary to these advertising promises, there is no workaday secret for that. Billy seems confounded that although he has rewritten the copy five times, his interlocutor (whose identity we never know) is laughing at him. Does he believe in the comments he has made about the route to absolute truth (about sports, no less), or is he merely spinning a message, 'Western Union Style'?

In another sequence (15) at his workplace, Billy is seen at a distance, almost anonymized, walking through a spare, modernist street scene, past Hushby's Steaks and Burgers. He is wearing a fashionable suit and dark glasses. A cigarette hangs from his lips. He enters an office building, where we discover he is directing a radio ad for Heinz Spaghetti Sauce. During this scene, we see Billy framed by the window of the recording booth facing the camera. In the foreground we see the backs of two boys sitting at microphones. On his cue, they begin to speak.

BOY 1: My spaghetti got neat tomato sauce.
BOY 2: Not neat, no. The flavour of Heinz Spaghetti Sauce would be described as mouth watering.

They continue to disagree until Billy interrupts:

BILLY: Boys, boys. All children love the taste of Heinz Spaghetti Sauce, right lads?
BOY 1: You keep out of this!

The script is clearly ridiculous and the actors laugh at the end, but Billy remains quite serious. This vision of food and family rings false – and is entirely different from Billy and Antoinette's own meals – but, presumably, Billy has written it. Again a distinction is highlighted between scripted and unscripted media, as well as between advertising discourse and observational cinema.

By comparison, the 'real' inserts itself much more forcefully into the family's meals at home. For instance, in the middle of one of their dinnertime fights (scene 23), Bogart interjects his own response to the family dynamic. Ignored when he requests a fork and later a ride on his father's back, Bogart finally gets his parents' attention when he tells them about a bowel movement he has made on the kitchen floor. 'Bring me that piece of shit,' says Billy, without missing a beat. To Billy's genuine surprise, Bogart brings it over. This scene is one that would never be found in a scripted film and could never have been planned, even in an unscripted one. Nevertheless, with great psychoanalytic resonance, Bogart's parents continue discussing acquisition of objects as a way to convey their emotions about the relationship. Antoinette says, 'We need a washer and dryer. But I don't want to panic about that until we have another kid.' Moments later she contradicts herself by saying, 'I don't know how long I'll last with you.' She eats with gusto despite the emotionally tense scene and the excrement in the kitchen.

During another meal (scene 16) Billy announces a 'new regime,' a program of 'discipline, sensitivity, warmth, understanding, cleanliness, friendship.' 'You,' he announces to Antoinette, 'are 80% of it.' 'Oh no! You're not doing it to me,' she playfully protests. The cleanliness, Billy clarifies, is to be emotional and spiritual; he jokes that it will be achieved through the sprinkling around of a 'spiritual lux,' an ironic comment on consumer products. Although playful, this scene, too, highlights the incursion of advertising discourse into everyday intimacy.

One of the aspects of fascination with the film concerns the willing-

Antoinette Edwards. Courtesy Allan King Films Ltd.

Billy Edwards. Courtesy Allan King Films Ltd.

Bogart Edwards. Courtesy Allan King Films Ltd.

ness of the Edwardses to participate. This issue is confronted headlong in a 'backstage' scene (11), where the two talk about their desires for fame while lounging on Antoinette's bed. Billy enumerates his desires: success, money, fame. 'Fame is what I want more than anything else. Fame.' He then asserts that Antoinette wants the same things. She disagrees, but then says, 'I want men and women alike to say "I love her. Why couldn't I be more like that?" I want guys to really crave me.' In this scene, their desires for fame and adoration are clearly expressed, addressing head on their decision to participate in the film.

In a number of the scenes described above, *A Married Couple* engages directly with the promotional aspect of subjectivity in late capitalism. In a study of 1960s film portraits in both documentary and the avant-garde, Paul Arthur argues that 'all film portraits are in part advertisements, declarations of the quiddity, if not the commodification, of their subjects.'[2] This connection between quiddity, or essence, and commodity speaks to a situation where subjects must be able to sell themselves both on the labour market and in the realm of intimacy. The family could no longer be perceived as a zone of safety away from the debasements of labour. The domestic realm was simply another sphere where value was assessed and prices paid. In the wake of self-sufficient family units, the only thing keeping the family together was the inertia of traditions. Paradoxically, the rejection of such outmoded moral systems often led to the embrace of commodification as the basis for human contact.[3]

A Married Couple directly engages with this paradox. As an advertising executive, Billy is openly involved with the crafting of consumer society. One of the primary topics of conversation between the couple concerns the acquisition of material goods. Part of their problem – one that has not gone away – is the issue of human connection and value in a marketplace. *Husband, wife, man, woman, father, mother* – the words are so freighted as to be almost uninhabitable. Even the word *adult* itself was on the way out.[4]

Just as the contradictions of married life become apparent through this kind of filmmaking, so, too, the strong language in the film, normal in people's lives but taboo in filmic representation of the time, underscores its status as a documentary. In the second scene of the film, a morning sequence, Antoinette calls Billy for breakfast while he is upstairs shaving, and his response transgresses the contemporary possibility of television and propels the film into the realm of reality: 'I heard you ... Fuck it! I'll come down when I'm ready.' The use of 'foul language' was one of the issues confronted in the attempt to attain approval for the film from the Ontario Censor Board. The board delayed release of the film, demanding cuts. 'Eventually,' says King, 'I gave them four "fucks" and a "cunt." The original text was restored for all other usage anywhere.'[5] Although the language is perhaps unremarkable today, it would have been inconceivable in a 'scripted' drama of the period. The documentary aspect of the film permits the use of 'real' speech, which turned out to be one of the main topics considered by critics.

The second controversy spawned by the film concerns a nude bathing sequence during their vacation (scene 17). Guitar music accompanies a long shot showing a car driving along a country road. The sun is shining and the late summer colours are breathtaking. A dissolve transforms the scene to green reeds against sparkling blue water. The distinctive call of a loon is heard. As the camera zooms out, an empty rowboat completes the scene of eastern North American cottage life. In this bucolic retreat, a site of emotional cleanliness, Billy and Antoinette have apparently been able to reconnect. A shot of a bed on a cabin floor from the head, shows them waking up and embracing. Merton walks into the frame, filling it with his wagging tail. The camera pans right to reveal Bogart on a neighbouring mattress. Bogart awakens and climbs into bed between his parents. Billy and Antoinette agree that they 'need more romanticism.' This apparent substitution of 'romanticism' for 'romance' is corroborated in the next scene in which the three are seen through the reeds bathing naked in the sparkling lake together, an image of Eden. A soft, appealing light washes over them all, giving an almost Impressionist patina to the scene. Yet the nudity, however painterly and romantic, raised concerns for the Censor Board.

By contrast, and somewhat ironically, the drama created by suggestions of Antoinette's infidelity were not particularly controversial. During the party scene (18), which follows the cottage episode, there is a five-minute sequence in which we see Antoinette flirting with an unidentified man. The conversation is condensed, something we can glean because the background sounds change, but its jumpiness succeeds in making us aware of the excitement of the two participants. They discuss their private lives, marriages, and living arrangements. A lengthy extreme close-up shows him taking his wedding ring on and off, while she fusses with a tassel on her dress.

Billy, noticeably upset, moves through the party taking photos. The seven-shot sequence of picture taking provides a self-reflexive comment on the filmmaking process going on at the party. In a sound bridge, we hear Antoinette saying, 'you can never really satisfy another person ... I can't provide specific things for Billy. There's a lot of people in the world.' 'Why do you have to have them all?' asks her conversational partner. 'Not all of them,' she says. 'But why do you have to have just one?'

The sequence that follows (scene 19) is made up entirely of an extreme close-up of Antoinette's and Billy's faces. 'In diesen heil'gen Hallen,' a bass aria from Mozart's opera *The Magic Flute* on the record player accompanies the image of Antoinette crying while they embrace.[6] He asks her something and she shakes her head 'no' while the camera zooms in on her face. There is a cut to a shot from over her shoulder. Now she is nodding 'yes.' This sequence of emotional turmoil and an extended embrace foreshadows the final scene of the film in which they cling together, exhausted. This image, much circulated as promotion for the film, encapsulates in a single action the couple's difficult relationship.

The text of the famous aria, sung by Sarastro to Pamina, speaks of forgiveness and love.

Within these hallowed halls
One knows not revenge.
And should a person have fallen,
Love will guide him to duty.
Then wanders he on the hand of a friend
Cheerful and happy into a better land.

Within these hallowed walls,
Where human loves the human,
No traitor can lurk,
Because one forgives the enemy.
Whomever these lessons do not please,
Deserves not to be a human being.[7]

The sentiment of reconciliation in the aria is unmistakable, but the ability of Antoinette and Billy to live up to these Enlightenment ideals is uncertain.

Despite this momentary lull, like a show of fireworks the film climaxes in a series of spectacular fights. Antoinette and Billy's disagreement ranges over a number of by now familiar themes and brings them to another level of incivility. Bogart is shown lying in his crib, looking at a book, while his parents are downstairs arguing. (The repeated cutaways to Bogart throughout the film also allow for a reading of the relationship through his eyes, which might help to explain its almost absurd

Antoinette and Billy embrace. Courtesy Allan King Films Ltd.

This close-up was widely used as promotion for the film. Courtesy
Allan King Films Ltd.

level of affective intensity.) Billy, a parody of the post-war patriarch, is in his red underwear holding a pipe. The discussion escalates until, finally, Billy pulls rank, yelling, 'I'm the one that goes to work. I'm the one who goes down there and draws the money that pays for this place and everything in it.' Antoinette accuses Billy of treating her like a servant, saying, 'you expect me to be at your beck and call. You never said "thank you" once in your Whole. Damn. Life.' Billy repeatedly insists that he should be primary in the relationship, as he supports their life: 'I don't want your goddamn emotions spilling all over me in the morning.' But he also insists that he does everything for her. At the same time, he claims that their relationship has 'nothing to do with power.' Antoinette voices her concerns that he will lose his job. Although he insists that he is 'doing very well,' it becomes clear that he has lost a series of jobs and isn't always employed. The earlier scene of him at work includes some one telling him to rewrite his copy for a sixth time.

The scene is interrupted by the ringing of the telephone. Antoinette jumps up to answer it. We watch her in long shot in the dining room, as though on a stage. She is laughing and her tone has completely changed from the dramaturgy of her marriage. She hangs up the phone, and in a shot redolent of the best observational cinema we see her face change from relaxation and delight to a bitter expression suited to the fight in the living room, to which she returns after a detour to the kitchen. Although he presses her, she won't say who was on the phone. 'Hey. You be careful, eh?' says Billy, and it is possible to read his comment either as a threat or as genuine concern.

As the film works up to a climax, Antoinette expresses the paradox of their married state, 'I just figure it's never going to be anything marvellous between us. And if we change for someone else, it's probably going to be the same with them. So the best thing is stop dreaming about it being wonderful. And if you can stand the sight of each other, put up with it and try to make a life out of it. That's all.' As the conversation continues in the living room in the final scene of the film, Antoinette suggests living on different floors and co-parenting, but Billy disagrees, saying they should move apart.

BILLY: I don't want a three room house.

ANTOINETTE: I'd rather have a three room house that works than a nine room house that's full of shit.

BILLY: You don't want to be married.

ANTOINETTE: No, I don't.

BILLY: You can't have it all … The framework isn't the problem. The laws of society are not the problem in this marriage. The problem is you and me … What we don't know is if we really hate one another or not.

She reaches into his jumpsuit and picks at some blackheads. He pushes her away, annoyed. He strokes her nose aggressively, then lifts her up and hugs her limp body. The camera zooms out and guitar music comes up on the soundtrack as he rocks her through the credit sequence. Finally, he tries to lift her. 'Come on,' he says. There is no response from her as the shot fades out.

The film ends on this unresolved note, leaving the audience to presume that the relationship is almost as exhausted as its participants. Seeing this particular marriage reach a new level of crisis has the potential to make the audience question the status of the entire institution, despite Billy's assertion that the problem is between the two of them. Do the performances in the film relate to psychodrama? Given the playing out of the emotional intensities of the relationship for the camera, elements of therapeutic psychodrama are clearly present. At work also is the influence of Living Theatre, here investigating the social frames around domesticity and documentary itself. But given that the experiment of observational cinema in the home was done for the purposes of the film, not for the participants, and that the audience was not directly confronted in the experience, perhaps the related claims of melodrama are the strongest.

Melodrama is a genre devoted to exploring the particular knot of contradictions at the heart of domestic life; most often this occurs through peeping at and eavesdropping on the private domestic lives of its characters. Soap opera and melodrama alike are usually referred to in derogatory ways, most likely because of their focus on the domestic, a devalued feminine realm, and because of their characteristic emphasis on talk over action. The spectacle of the private realm is probably part of its scandalous allure. Melodrama has often been assessed as a genre for women in patriarchy, as the focus is always the misery of wasted and underappreciated lives, no doubt a common feeling for wives and mothers. In relation to this *A Married Couple* demonstrates both conti-nuity and difference. Antoinette can certainly be seen as a subject of patriarchal oppression. She is entirely reliant upon her husband and his income. Everything she wants must first be approved by him, and many of the discussions in the film centre on Billy's thwarting of her ac-quisitive desires. She is shown to be constantly subjected to unwanted sexual advances and during one fight she is physically abused.

However, Billy appears equally flummoxed by the relationship. He, too, is shown to be suffering from the pressures of patriarchy in which he is expected to fulfil a masculine role of perfect reason and com-mand impossible for a mere mortal. Both are shown to be failing or, put differently, the institution of marriage is failing both. In this way, the observational aspect overrules the conventions of melodrama. We are asked to look at what is really going on, rather than to assume either character's position exclusively. In this way the film 'acts as a Rorschach test,' ultimately asking us challenging questions about ourselves and our assumptions and about the conventions of both film and marriage.[8]

Thomas Elsaesser has argued that melodrama is characterized by the

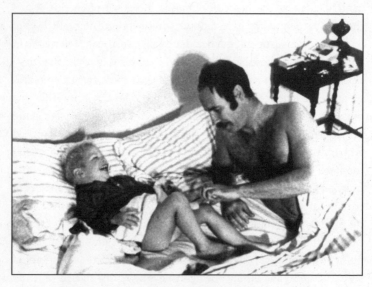

Bogart and Billy. Courtesy Allan King Films Ltd.

sublimation of dramatic conflict into 'décor, colour, gesture and com-
position of frame, which in the best melodramas is perfectly thematized
in terms of the characters' emotional and psychological predicaments.'[9]
In other words, although melodrama is a genre based on talk, often
things cannot be expressed. They must be observed in the *mise en scène*.
As Sarah Kozloff puts it, 'Dialogue in melodramas functions to reveal
feelings, and it does so through a heightened, even overblown, rhetori-
cal style.' At the same time, 'melodramas – which seem so verbally over-
explicit – actually hinge around the not said, the words that cannot be
spoken.'[10] Observations of environment and the not-said function in *A
Married Couple* teach viewers to look for subtext, even in documentary.[11]

In melodrama, the range of strong action is quite limited. The real
world recedes in the face of the overwhelming emotions of the characters. Characters become one another's sole referent: 'there is no world
outside to be acted on, no reality that could be defined or assumed
unambiguously.' Characters' behaviour is 'often pathetically at variance
with the real objectives they want to achieve. A sequence of substitute
actions creates a kind of vicious circle in which the close nexus of cause
and effect is somehow broken and – in an often overtly Freudian sense
– displaced.'[12] Indeed *A Married Couple* is something of a primer in reading displacements and condensations in intimate life.

In many ways, including its setting in the middle-class home, *A Married Couple* fits exceedingly well with the genre of melodrama. The 'setting of the family melodrama almost by definition is the middle-class
home, filled with objects, which ... surround the heroine in a hierarchy
of apparent order that becomes increasingly suffocating.'[13] The middle-
class home could be said to be the chronotope or defining spatio-tem-
porality of the melodrama; a space in which time feels as though it has
been arrested and the outside world has disappeared. Vivian Sobchack
has shown how Russian literary theorist Mikhail Bakhtin's notion of the
chronotope can be used to analyse films noirs. Sobchack persuasively ar-

gues that the spaces in which the action of these B-films of the 1940s and 1950s take place 'materially ground both the internal logic of the films and the external logic of the culture and allow each to be intelligible in terms of the other.' This premise about the grounding of genre films in what she calls 'the extratextual life-world' seems to hold even more strongly for a film set in the 'real' material conditions of its characters.[14]

The 'characteristic attempt of the bourgeois household to make time stand still, immobilise life and fix forever domestic property relations as the model of social life and a bulwark against the more disturbing sides in human nature' is amply illustrated in *A Married Couple*. Not only are all markers of the passing of time obscured in the film, but it is precisely the claustrophobia of the accumulation of things that creates some of the drama and expressive *mise en scène*. Writes Elsaesser, 'pressure is generated by things crowding in on [the characters], life becomes increasingly complicated because [it is] cluttered with obstacles and objects that invade their personalities, take them over, stand for them, become more real than the human relations or emotions they were intended to symbolise.'[15] The drama that pervades *A Married Couple* through its characters is one of attaining authenticity in the face of materialism.

Unlike the doomed domestic relations of melodrama (the timing is always off; the opportunities are already missed), *A Married Couple* explores the striving for authentic meaning in the face of social changes and promotional subjectivities. Yet, as Elsaesser shows, in some ways these issues are the time-worn themes of the middle class. He characterizes classic melodrama as social change understood in 'private contexts and emotional terms.'[16] This apt definition helps us to understand the personalization of the political in the 1960s. Not only was 'the personal is political' a rallying cry of feminist consciousness raising, but the 'politics of the image,' identified by Daniel Boorstin, proposed that politics itself was taking on melodramatic form.[17] Politicians were becoming celebrities and their personal lives were recorded and scrutinized like soap operas. One way to put it is that the personalization of politics, long found in bourgeois art forms such as melodrama, came into its own in that decade as a modality for experiencing everyday life.

A Married Couple traces the struggles of a family attempting to find answers in a world from which meaning is being stripped. The circularity of everyday distress becomes a defining feature and, paradoxically, an emotional touchstone, providing something of the consistency and structure that is lacking everywhere else. Similarly, their own awareness of their performance as a married couple denaturalizes their lives and by extension the demands of the institution. The end product is the result of these various levels of shaping, from the performance to the filming, directing, and editing, all of which combine to make something *both* true *and* mediated. In this sense, it may be said that the film brings to light certain of the unwritten scenarios of the family that Laing identified, and that it offers insight into both the performance of self in everyday life and the on- and offstage personae of the actors. In this, it is a melodrama that at once satisfies genre conventions and offers them back to us as scripts for everyday life.

As we join the action in progress (and there are very few establishing shots and no explanatory text or indications of timeline), the story takes on a repetitive, circular structure, not unlike a dream. Like a spiral, the first scene, although a disagreement, is spirited and seemingly light-hearted, while in the last, Antoinette and Billy seem to have come to the end of their ability to engage. They are at the end of discourse, exhausted. What we witness in the interim is a married couple performing, as much for each other as for the camera. The question of the ambiguity of social roles is a recurring theme. How to act as a mother, wife, father, husband, adult man, or adult woman is never clear. The 'theatrical stages' of home and work and of socializing provide only hazy parameters of appropriate behaviour. Their desires are entirely organized by consumer culture, fittingly the same arena in which Billy works. The value of the keyboard over which they fight several times, seems moot, as the actually existing piano in their home is never shown being played. The structure of the family has broken down, but nothing has yet replaced it. The scene of the bacchanal at the isolated farmhouse shows the chaos of life without convention, but does not provide a meaningful alternative for day-to-day living. So they are thrown back to discussing renovation of their spaces and the magical thinking of 'spiritual lux.'

One of the significant insights of the film is a delineation of the pre-greased grooves down which bourgeois couples inexorably move, despite any given family's feeling of its own uniqueness. This insight is paradoxically achieved through generic convention rather than sociology. *A Married Couple* documents, in its way, the interpenetration of life with melodramatic convention. Whereas melodramas are designed to help viewers work through the contradictions of their own lives, this documentary melodrama refuses to resolve the contradictions and potentially demands from its audience a radical rethinking of domestic bliss. We are never allowed the dodge of fiction. If this is a real family, then the problems it confronts us with are not over at the end. They are the ones they – and perhaps we – continue to live with.

We are indeed shown things in this version of intimate family life that would fall outside the possibility of fiction in the period. For one, the film is full of swearing, nudity, and the discussion of excrement, all captured in ways that would be impossible in a scripted film and during which scenes the participants do indeed appear to go 'off book.' What they are performing has no precursor in filmed drama. These are moments in which the film's form as documentary delivers the spontaneity of unscripted reality. The risk-taking originality and unflinching vision of the film led to a range of critical responses, which are the subject of the next chapter.

Promotion and Reception

As discussed in the last chapter, the combination of observational footage and crafted narrative make *A Married Couple* into a remarkable and unrepeatable achievement. It sparked a good deal of discussion, and no small amount of controversy, when it was released in the fall of 1969.

With a budget of more than $200,000, *A Married Couple* was not a cheap film by Canadian standards. Aquarius Films, King's production company, made a concerted attempt to market the film, spending an additional $30,000. Advertisements featuring a posed photograph of the Edwards family semi-clad, a naked Bogart front and centre and a tasteful nude pose of Antoinette, back to the camera, appeared in newspapers across Canada.[1] Across the bottom of the poster appeared the words 'the Jones they're not,' and in small font above the cinema information appeared the disclaimer mandated by the Ontario Censor Board: 'the language in this film might offend some people.' Judging by newspaper advertisements in a number of urban papers, *A Married Couple* emerged alongside and competed for cinema audiences with films such as *Easy Rider* (1969), *Take the Money and Run* (1969), *Midnight Cowboy* (1969), *I Am Curious (Yellow)* (1967), *Monterey Pop* (1968), *Marlowe* (1969), *Paint Your Wagon* (1969), *My Night at Maud's* (1969), *Valérie* (1969), *The Mini-Skirt Mob* (1968), *The Killing of Sister George* (1968), *Butch Cassidy and the Sundance Kid* (1969), *Medium Cool* (1969), and *Oliver!* (1968).

In Toronto, *A Married Couple* premiered on 6 November 1969 at Cinecity at an invitation-only screening. The next day it opened to the public with six shows daily. After a cut-back to three screenings a day in December, it closed on 20 January 1970, but was followed by one-week runs at the Park Cinema (30 January–6 February) and the Crest Cinema (6–13 February). It opened on 2 February 1970 at Kips Bay Theatre in New York , where it was given six screenings per day until the week of 18 February. In Montreal, *A Married Couple* opened on 12 November 1969 with seven shows daily at Cinéma Guy. It closed on 14 January 1970. In Vancouver, *A Married Couple* opened in February 1970 at the Famous Players Denman Place Theatre. In London, England, *A Married Couple* played at the Paris Pullman Cinema in December 1970.

The Edwardses, who had been granted veto on any of the footage, but not on the finished film, promoted the film like celebrities and attended the Toronto premiere.[2] Their turn as film stars catapulted them onto the society pages, at least in the short term. A picture of Antoinette and Billy atop a stuffed horse was featured in the *Toronto Telegram*'s New Year's column by Gillian Robertson. 'Over on Rushton Ave.[*sic*], the Married Couple, Billy and Antoinette Edwards, presented a lovely evening for their friends, full of uncomplicated elegance. Antoinette wore a blue shiny gown with an empire waist and low neckline. Billy wore a crepe shirt with floppy ruffles at the neck and sleeves. Their son Bogart, 4, while he was up, wore a frilly blue shirt and velvet jerkin and bell-bottoms.'[3]

Accepted to the director's fortnight at Cannes and opened to theatrical release after being rejected by commissioning network CTV, *A Married Couple* was greeted with markedly – and significantly – mixed reviews. For many, the film heralded the arrival of Canadian cinema. For instance, writing in the *Toronto Daily Star*, Dorothy Mikos called it 'undoubtedly the most important feature film made in Canada to date ... It brings to the screen a level of realism and raw emotion that seems to make professional acting an unbearable sham.'[4] In the *New York Times*,

Promotional poster for the film. Courtesy Allan King Films Ltd.

Clive Barnes called it 'quite simply one of the greatest movies I have ever seen' and cited it as a sign that 'Toronto is no longer the conservative city of good, gray British imperialism it once was.'[5] *Time* magazine listed *A Married Couple* as one of the ten best films of 1970.[6]

Reviewers suggested an awareness of the film's novelty. In *Saturday Night*, Marshall Delany characterized *A Married Couple* as

> a rich, many-levelled experience. The implications of its technique and its subject matter are so vast that it may well turn out to be one of those endlessly seminal films – for instance, it may affect the documentary film in the 1970s the way *Citizen Kane* affected the fiction film of the 1940s and 1950s ... This is the age of exhibitionism and the age of therapy, and it is obvious that Billy and Antoinette are nothing if not of their period ... But what remains most important about *A Married Couple* – the factor that, I suspect, will cause it to be studied in university film courses decades from now – is the subtle changes it produces in relationships that, in this period, have grown ever more shaky. Artist and art. Creator and character. Actor and part. *A Married Couple* rearranges them all.[7]

Writing in New York's *East Village Other*, Lita Eliscu was effusive: 'It is difficult to review a film so directly about other human beings whose life has not been stylized, dramatized, metamorphosed and rendered harmless by the action of time, other culture, or anything else ... As no other film before its time, this one requires its audience. Reactions to *A Married Couple* are foremost emotional and only secondarily aesthetic ... The startling poignancy of the events shown are not 2-dimensional fictions and the purpose of acting here is to save lives. As I learn more about me, so I realize more of Billy and Antoinette Edwards.'[8]

But many influential critics were less sympathetic. Writing in the *Toronto Telegram*, Clyde Gilmour listed *A Married Couple* as one of top ten letdowns of the year.[9] Pauline Kael, the famously judgmental *New Yorker* critic, wrote: 'Recording the antagonisms in an actual marriage yields much less decisive revelations than conventional dramatic techniques do, and to the question of whether the quality of these revelations is such as to outweigh the tediousness and the unresolved complications the answer in this case, I think, is no ... *A Married Couple* is not too much, it's too little.'[10]

Vincent Canby wrote in the *New York Times*: 'The unreality prompted by the camera's presence is acknowledged in the film, which then proceeds to pass off this conscious performance as some kind of meta-truth that is neither fact nor fiction. What King ultimately proves, I think, is that something that is neither fact nor fiction is less meta-truth than sophisticated sideshow.'[11]

In the *Village Voice*, Molly Haskell asserted that *A Married Couple* demonstrated the de-eroticization of the human environment as diagnosed by Herbert Marcuse and Rollo May:

In King's film, an educated, middle-class, vaguely liberated and moderately aware couple argue about money and their marriage, walk around in the nude, eat dinner in their underwear, pick their teeth, say fuck, make love, go skinny-dipping with their son. It is a depressing exhibition and the most de-eroticized environment this side of a New York cocktail party ... Antoinette and Billy Edwards open their pockets inside out, and nothing falls on the floor... The fact that they would allow the film to be made – that they have so little of themselves to keep from each other, and therefore little between them to keep from the world – tells more about them than all their raw harangues. As they argue, it is obvious that their problems have nothing to do with money or furniture or even marriage, that their bids for power arise from their own insubstantial egos, from a shaky sense of self.[12]

The film troubled categories and disturbed some reviewers' sense of propriety. Genres were disrupted and viewers didn't know how they ought to react. As Louis Marcorelles asked in *Le Monde*, 'Où commence, où finit la comédie?'[13] Ronald Blumer put the problem succinctly: '[*A Married Couple*] is a frequently painful, often funny, embarrassingly intimate portrait of a couple whose marriage is breaking up. Although it is not a staged film, it is photographed in colour with the same clarity and sensitivity of a studio job; though not a fictional film, it is often more dramatic than anything that could have come from a screenwriter's pen. Allan King, who with *Warrendale* had shown himself to be one of Canada's most talented filmmakers has done it again, and this time with a movie that is so interesting in so many ways that one hardly knows were to begin talking about it.'[14]

Some, like *Time* magazine, opted to call it a documentary: 'a brutally frank documentary... an unblinking dissection of the modern family... a perfect model of documentary film making.'[15] *Maclean's* averred, 'Allan King has snatched some incredibly intimate, agonizingly real moments from the lives of a suburban Toronto couple and assembled them into a magnificent documentary that turns the wide screen into a mirror for the audience. The film makes actors and scripts all but obsolete.'[16]

A number of reviewers distinguished between documentary and cinéma-vérité, inevitably touching on the issue of performance. In a 1969 cover story in *Saturday Night* magazine, Marshall Delany wrote: 'These people, you begin to realize, are acting all the time – acting out, as it were. But what they are acting out is their own lives. *A Married Couple* pushes *cinéma vérité* to new frontiers of accomplishment; it also, in another way, pushes Method acting to a previously unimagined level.'[17] The *Saturday Review* saw in *A Married Couple* a new kind of cinema:

> The promise of *cinéma vérité* is that it holds the mirror up to nature without any refraction imposed by script or interpreters. Its problem is that the very presence of a camera and, later, the act of editing what the cam-

era has observed inevitably lead to some degree of distortion. Both the promise and the problem are fascinatingly apparent in Allan King's new film, *A Married Couple* ... But is it all really real? ... No, it can't all be really real. But if we accept *A Married Couple* as occupying a midway point between *vérité* and invention, the film seems far less problematical... Though they are not acting here in the conventional sense, they are most decidedly acting out – reiterating and replaying – the burdens and frustrations of their fractious relationship.[18]

Sight and Sound appreciated the film's subtle challenges:

The documentary camera, together with the documentary editor, can create innumerable fictions – and when *Married Couple* works, it is, for all the verisimilitude, on a *fictional* level. Possibly the facts are that for some of those ten weeks in 1968 the Edwards home was exactly like this; more interestingly, the film creates an example of raucous, flexible, and possibly normal marriage that has enough truth in it to relate to any number of other, more real marriages ... Whether or not their marriage was in fact ever like this, or might have been, it comes across on film, thanks to the ambiguity of Allan King's method, as all too plausible an experience.[19]

But Judith Crist called it 'pseudo-*cinéma vérité*' and Les Wedman wrote, 'King didn't convince me that *A Married Couple* was either documentary or *cinéma vérité*.'[20] Their observations connected to widespread criticisms of the over-dramatization of reality, such as Clyde Gilmour's commentary in the *Toronto Telegram*: 'My own quarrel with *A Married Couple* is not over its blunt dialogue but over the fact that I simply cannot believe that the Edwards EVER completely forgot the camera and the microphone in the way that the distressed youngsters of *Warrendale* obviously did. If my hunch is correct, what we're seeing in King's new film is not a completely candid and off-guard close-up of an authentic marriage in trouble, as the production purports to be, but to some extent a staged, calculated, louder-than-life "dramatization" of that marriage produced for public scrutiny.'[21] Similarly, *Newsweek* characterized it as 'a new kind of filmed psychodrama.'[22]

Many tried to understand the film in relation to other, mostly fictional films. *Variety* called it a cinéma-vérité 'street version' of *Who's Afraid of Virginia Woolf?* and *Faces*. Herbert Aronoff of the Montreal *Gazette* also made the link to Cassavetes, but proclaimed that '*Faces* ... probed the deeper abscesses of married life. *A Married Couple* doesn't and only annoys the viewer while the camera rolls on. *A Married Couple* is emasculated cinema. It has all the trappings of art but none of the power.'[23] In the *Globe and Mail* Martin Knelman observed that 'Billy and Antoinette treat the audience the way George and Martha treated the other couple in *Who's Afraid of Virginia Woolf?* – as shock absorbers.'[24]

By contrast, in *Maclean's* Larry Zolf wrote, 'Cassavetes' *Faces*, Antonioni's *La Notte*, Godard's *A Married Woman*, Lelouch's *A Man and Woman* ... evoked only a curious, detached sympathy. Watching *A Married Couple*, the audience is brutally involved ... *A Married Couple* is more than a nonfiction feature, more than mere psychodrama; it is a unique film experience.'[25]

Aside from the remarkable fact that the film was simultaneously lauded as a documentary and excoriated as a melodrama, for some the film's putatively excessive qualities were excuse for derision. For example, Vincent Canby implied that the film was a form of therapy – 'less expensive than analysis' was his phrase – of no interest to a wider audience. Canby described *A Married Couple* as 'a self-deceiving put-on,' calling the 'self-conscious intimacies' of *A Married Couple* 'unseemly.'[26] In this way, responses echoed those for melodrama in general, whose texts traditionally are found to be overly emotional, artificial, or otherwise excessive.

A number of commentators used the film to discuss issues of social norms, including privacy. Judith Crist called it 'peeping-Tom movie-making that is simply a bloody bore.'[27] In the *Toronto Daily Star*, Peter Harris speculated as to whether *A Married Couple* indicated 'a growing acceptance of invasion of privacy.'[28] Les Wedman wrote in the *Vancouver Sun*, 'In my square world husbands and wives don't fight or make love in public. Allan King's *A Married Couple* does, and if they don't mind exposing their innermost feelings and their most visible weaknesses for all to see, more power to them.'[29] Perhaps the most perceptive comment came from Martin Malina, who wrote in the *Montreal Star*: 'In *A Married Couple* life is imitating art ... The result may not be entirely candid but it is undeniably real ... Whether it is more or less "real" than "real life" is irrelevant; it is a masterful and highly innovative work of art and must be seen.'[30]

As these reviews indicate, the film crystallized a number of topical issues, including of the exposure of privacy, the state of documentary truth claims, and the status of performance. This range of responses was indicative of the timeliness of King's project. He used challenges to filmic conventions to engage with contemporary challenges to social conventions. In terms of both form and content, *A Married Couple* was the perfect embodiment of its experimental historical moment.

In an influential essay, 'Toward a Phenomenology of Nonfictional Film Experience,' Vivian Sobchack argues that, more than a film object or genre, documentary must be seen as a viewing position. Building on the work of French phenomenologist Jean-Pierre Meunier, Sobchack posits that there is a continuum from home movie to fiction film. In the former, the cinematic object is merely a mnemonic device for the viewer, who knows much more than the film reveals. In the latter, by contrast, the film is the extent of the information known about the fictional world, so each detail takes on heightened, even fetishistic, quality. In between, and mediating between the two, the documentary spectator engages in an 'apprenticeship' to the film object, in that 'our specific knowledge of these persons and events is contemporaneous with our viewing of the film.'[31]

However, while the home movie expects a longitudinal consciousness and the fiction film a lateral consciousness, the documentary demands something of both.

> Given my dependence upon it for information, the screen is less transparent than it is for me in the home movie – and, by virtue of the increased attention I must pay them so as to comprehend them specifically and accumulate them as a generality, images in the documentary experience gain in autonomy and intensity. Nonetheless, in that I have, from the first, posited the existence of what these images represent and am thus engaged in some degree of constitutive and evocative activity, the documentary image is not completely autonomous, but still connected to and intermediary between myself and what I perceive to be a 'real' unknown person or event 'in general.'[32]

Perhaps it was the feeling of flipping between these three modes of reception (incidentally identified by Meunier in 1969, the same year the film was made) that caused the reviewers some concern. *A Married Couple* is all three: a home movie, a documentary, and a fictional narrative. At different moments no doubt the film evokes varying responses from each individual viewer. In this, too, the response to the film confirms Sobchack's insistence on a phenomenological reading of documentary film. 'It is the viewer's consciousness that finally determines what kind of cinematic object it is.'[33]

Judging by the varied reactions canvassed above, to Sobchack's insights we must add that genre itself constitutes one of the key extra-textual horizons of expectation for viewers. An essential part of the experience of watching *A Married Couple* is to understand its emotional appeal in relation to either documentary or melodrama. Perhaps because of *A Married Couple*'s focus on emotion and the domestic sphere, it thwarted clear genre expectations about documentary. Yet in some ways *A Married Couple* represents just one of many experiments with the docufictional. The phenomenological and epistemological experience of documentary is the subject of the next chapter.

Imitation of Life? Towards a Theory of Documentary Mimesis

In a 1984 statement about the controversy over his film *Who's in Charge?*, 'More Muddy Morals: A Reply to Critics,' King wrote, '[artists and journalists] take in the experiences of other people (their lives, if you will), we chew them over, digest them, grunt and groan, and finally produce them in some formed expression. Now that describes something a lot more serious than voyeurism or manipulation. You could call it cannibalism.'[1] In making a film with and about real people, the dialogic aspect of cultural production – or cannibalism, if you will – is front and centre. The final film is not the product solely of the participants or the filmmakers, but is a complex and even bloody comingling of both. This interactive conception of cultural production adds complexity to the common pairing of reality with documentary and drama with fiction.

Engaging with reality on film has taken many forms, from re-enactment to performance and staging of various kinds with non-actors. Any notion of hybridity presumes a binary in which the initial terms are clearly distinct. But these definitions seem to exclude film texts such as *A Married Couple* that implicitly blur boundaries and confuse categories without clearly hybridizing any two recognized forms. The kind of response such texts evoke – and that *A Married Couple* provoked – has everything to do with their epistemological undecidability.

As can be seen from the reviews sampled in the last chapter, *A Married Couple* troubles categories. To understand the achievement of the film is, in no small sense, to understand its formal accomplishment, which makes some discussion of form warranted. In the main, the discussion of documentary/fiction hybridity tends along two docufictional lines: mockumentary and docudrama. In this chapter I consider how *A Married Couple* productively exceeds the discussion of these established hybridities.

An example of the difficulties one faces in defining the film can be seen in a perusal of the collection *Docufictions*. The editors, Gary Rhodes and John Parris Springer, map out the particular hybridities that exist between fiction and documentary. 'Late twentieth-century film culture has given rise to a rich corpus of hybrid texts which show, in increasingly self-conscious, even *generic* ways, the creative merging and synthesis of documentary and fictional narrative cinema.' According to them, documentaries are 'films about *real* people, places, and events,' told in distinctive styles, while fictional narratives have their own 'forms and devices of representation derived from literature and the theatre, including a more conscious attention to emplotment and characterization and a concern for the thematic or ideological significance of these elements organized through narrative structures and conventions of genre ... Fictional narratives involve the use of *invented* people, places and events.'[2] According to the binary they establish between documentary and fiction – reality and invention – two distinct hybrid forms may be created: mockumentary, a combination of documentary form with fictional content, and docudrama, a mix of fictional form with documentary content.

The categories devised by Rhodes and Springer simply do not apply to *A Married Couple*, a film in which, as we have seen, footage of ordinary people acting as themselves is crafted into a satisfying, albeit circular, dramatic structure. However, although terms such as 'fiction' and 'non-fiction' may not pertain, issues of performance, reality and fantasy certainly do. More complex than Rhodes and Springer's basic model of hybridity is Paula Rabinowitz's observation that cinéma-vérité and docudrama are 'two sides of the same representational coin: each depict[ing] history and subjectivity through vignettes of intimate life.'[3] William Rothman goes even further: 'What is fictional about a classical movie resides in its fiction that it is only fiction; what is fictional about a *cinéma vérité* film resides in its fiction that it is not fictional at all. Strip away what is fictional and there is no real difference between them.'[4] Vivian Sobchack's discussion of documentary phenomenology alluded to above attributes no small part of the meaning of the film to the act of reception. Yet, despite the observations by Rabinowitz, Rothman, and Sobchack about the continuities between fiction and non-fiction film, distinctions between reality and fantasy remain contentious aspects of media culture, particularly in the realm of reception.

In Canada, a number of docudramas have created telling controversies. *The Tar Sands* (1977), a docudrama about Alberta's oil patch, offended former premier, Peter Lougheed, who sued the CBC for defamation. Lougheed's lawyer stated, 'it's either news or drama but obviously this shows that mixing the two doesn't work.'[5] Controversies have erupted also over John Smith's representation of abuse in the Catholic Church in *The Boys of St. Vincent* (1991) and the documentary series by Brian McKenna about Canada's participation in the Second World War, *The Valour and the Horror* (1992). In all cases, the controversies emerged because of the allegedly contentious interpretation of events, often signalled by fact-fiction hybridity on topical matters, or in the case of *The Valour and the Horror*, historical events with major national significance.[6]

In media studies, authors tend to focus on one or the other of these hybrid genres. *Faking it*, for example, is an essential study of the mockumentary. *No Other Way to Tell It*, by Derek Paget, *Real Emotional Logic* by Steve Lipkin, and *Why Docudrama?*, a collection edited by long-time observer of documentary Alan Rosenthal, all consider the cultural presence of docudrama. The studies in this category tend to focus on television, long a hybridizer of cultural forms. As Raymond Williams noted in the introduction to his famous study *Television: Technology and Cultural Form* (1974), an 'intrinsic element of television [is] its capacity to enter a situation and show what is actually happening in it.' For Williams, the result is an 'overlap between what is classified as factual report and what is classified as dramatic presentation.' In this sense, television formally engages in 'a rethinking and reworking of the conventional distinction between reality and fiction.'[7]

The quintessential televisual form is the docudrama (or the drama-doc in the United Kingdom), a genre that blends fact and fiction. As Derek Paget shows, docudramas supplement the factual record with the emotional realism demanded by the television viewing experience. Expressing television's 'historic popular mission' to inform and amuse, dramadocs embody television's objective 'to weld the twin aims of education and entertainment into one.' Dramadocs are successful, Paget argues, because 'the camera's ability to go anywhere and see anything is both borrowed from documentary on behalf of the drama and extended by the drama on behalf of the documentary.'[8]

In the British tradition, dramadocs review or celebrate events of national or international significance, represent the careers of noteworthy figures or ordinary citizens thrust onto the public stage, and portray issues of concern to national or international communities in order to provoke discussion.[9] In the United States, by contrast, the docudrama has come to be known as the 'trauma drama,' in which an ordinary person struggles against the social institutions that restrict his or her rights.[10] This hybridization has particular resonance in Britain because of the strength of its documentary tradition. Where documentary has connotations of seriousness and has often been associated with masculine tastes and topics, drama is often considered more frivolous (especially when attached to the prefix melo-) and is associated with feminine tastes and topics.[11] Docudrama, then, hybridizes not only two forms, but two sets of tastes and often two visions of the world as well. The combination is likened to a feminizing of the public sphere and its more serious political representatives, such as the documentary. However, as Paget notes, even when drama fills in the factual record, the prevailing form of docudrama emphasizes social realism and naturalistic acting. Therefore, although docudrama is a hybrid, it does not stretch the possibilities of hybridizing fact and fiction very far.

In his book *Documentary Television in Canada* (2002), David Hogarth notes that docudrama has been an integral part of Canadian broadcast history, but not as a result of the documentary tradition imported from the British film movement. He argues that the Canadian tradition came directly from radio. By the mid-1930s Canadian radio producers had come to view 'documentary programming as a uniquely educational, entertaining and efficient way of telling stories about the nation.' After the advent of television broadcasting in Canada in 1952, dramatizations and docudrama were well respected, he notes, as extensions of both information services and fictional storytelling from CBC radio. Hogarth argues that, distinct from the film tradition nurtured at the National Film Board, television documentary inherited from radio a personalized form of address. For example, television documentary featured subject-driven stories and often used hosts to mediate between audience and broadcaster. Both of these textual strategies served to make television's public service fare less intimidating and more popular.[12]

Although re-enactment also made a virtue of the necessities of low budgets and cumbersome filmmaking technology, according to Hogarth re-enactments were not considered less real or less effective than other forms of fact-based television. On the contrary, it was hoped that they were objects of visual pleasure, 'spectacle[s] that viewers might long to see.' Images and sounds produced in studio could be made to maximize the dramatic effect on rudimentary television sets with low resolution. Also, dramatizations could be versioned in both French and English, a clear advantage for a fledgling public broadcaster trying to provide service in two languages. The CBC took seriously its role of putting Canada on screen as an imagined community that would induce excitement in viewers.[13]

Nevertheless, the use of this form of address in the new domestic medium of television led to familiar cultural anxieties about the blurring of masculine and feminine spheres and aesthetics.[14] While Paget notes that the blurring of documentary and drama can lead to cultural anxiety about the diminished capacity to perceive the difference, he argues that audiences are accustomed to these hybrid forms. He points out that 'fact-fiction forms are a special preserve of the mass medium of television,' one that audiences become conversant in quite quickly.[15] Despite the arguments about audience comprehension, docudramas have served as significant media events, both in Canada and abroad. Often they have courted controversy – not only because of their subject matter. The hybrid form has frequently meant that the controversies become epistemological, challenging the information put forward as interpretation inadequately signalled, rather than fact.

Although funded in part by CTV, *A Married Couple* was not ultimately released on television. Paradoxically, television might have been a more natural home for this 'actuality drama.' However, as is clear from this brief overview, *A Married Couple* does not fit neatly into either of the usual televisual hybrids, docudrama or mockumentary, for one simple reason: it does not engage in the realm of re-enactment. Its performances are illocutionary, and in this sense real. What happened in the pro-filmic performances had implications for the performers beyond the scene filmed.

For this reason, it is not exactly neo-realism either. Neo-realist style derives from the experiments of Italian cinema in the latter half of the

1940s. Films such as *Rome, Open City* (1945), *Paisan* (1946), and *Bicycle Thieves* (1948) featured real people, often non-professional actors, in roles and situations similar to those they may have experienced during the extreme conditions of the Second World War and its devastating aftermath. Reality, particularly the experiences of real people, took on a new significance. Matching the filmmakers' concerns, films were often shot on location, using real argot and dialect. The result was a sense of reality combined with the satisfactions of good fiction.

Neo-realism is arguably a hybrid form because of its reliance upon 'real people' rather than professional actors signifying authenticity with their artless self-presentation. Of course, neo-realists in Italy and elsewhere have also used professional actors and the form's purity is routinely questioned. In any event, such non-professional actors are placed into scenarios written and directed by professional filmmakers. In this way, neo-realism parallels the practice in classical documentary of ordinary people 'acting to play themselves.'[16] This well-entrenched aspect of documentary performance is often left out of discussions of hybridity in documentary form. Before the advent of the interview, and well before the ideology of spontaneous truth, documentaries routinely portrayed ordinary people acting in scenes devised by film-makers to represent typical situations. Filmed in 35 mm, many early documentaries featured scenes that were rehearsed and shot in numerous takes. Wooden acting by participants was often a badge of authenticity.

From the outset, then, there arguably existed a normative aspect of reality-based media. What was being shown were people's habits and routines, ordinary people performing in ways very similar to their everyday lives. In this sense, the melodramatic phrase taken from the Douglas Sirk movie of the same name (itself taken from Aristotle's definition of drama) is à *propos*: these films were the 'imitation of life.' To imitate life is already to have a conception of it, formed through study or observation. This is the conceptual shape into which filmable facts are organized.

What might it mean to define the documentary impulse along these mimetic lines, as an imitation of life? To do so, we might turn to the German tradition of cultural criticism. Rather than espouse a simple theory of film as reproduction of life, Siegfried Kracauer, for example, argued for film's potential to redeem the physical world.[17] According to Kracauer, film is both a sign and a symptom of technological modernity and a potential means by which human experience in modernity might be revealed in a new way. Film's 'affinity' to the world, its mimetic aspect, 'includes both film's ability to record and its potential to reveal something in relation to that world.' According to Miriam Bratu Hansen, 'Kracauer participates in an alternative tradition that locates the film experience in psychic regions closer to those explored by Freud in *Beyond the Pleasure Principle* (1920), particularly through concepts of shock, primary masochism, and the death drive ... Kracauer [seems] interested in the possibilities of masochistic self-abandonment and dissociation, in the cinema's ability to subject the viewer, in an institutionally bounded form of play, to encounters with contingency, lack of control, and otherness.' Hansen believes that Kracauer is interested in the difference between discourse, where our habits of seeing hold sway, and the contingency of a material reality that always threatens the dissolution of meaning.[18] This perspective shows a certain vein of cinema to be a precursor to the televisual tendency to bring reality together with textual convention. Insofar as *A Married Couple* indicates the discursive organization of melodrama in our perception of reality, it also possibly challenges the expectations of genre. In addition, the film engages with the deeper sense of reality as replete with fantasy and performance.

It seems particularly significant that in *Theory of Film* (1960) Kracauer chooses as an example of the most revealing film possible the twenty-four-hour, real-time, uncut surveillance of a couple. Kracauer writes that the painter and filmmaker Fernand Léger

> dreamed of a monster film which would have to record painstakingly the life of a man and a woman during twenty-four consecutive hours: their work, their silence, their intimacy. Nothing should be omitted; nor should they ever be aware of the presence of the camera ... Such a film would not just portray a sample of everyday life but, in portraying it, dissolve the familiar contours of that life and expose what our conventional notions of it conceal from view – its widely ramified roots in crude existence. We might well shrink, panic-stricken, from these alien patterns which would denote our ties with nature and claim recognition as part of the world we live in and are.

Kracauer's postulation about the potential fascination and horror at the heart of the unseen mundane and everyday supports his view that film is at its most successful when it uses found stories, slight plots, the episodic 'border region' between fiction and non-fiction, and real or real-seeming people. 'The preference for real people on the screen and the documentary approach seem to be closely interrelated.'[19]

In her extrapolation of Kracauer's film theory, Hansen identifies that for him cinema operates as the site of a popular form of modernism. She argues that people seek out the shocks and attractions of the movie theatre as one way to experience a controlled version of the upheavals and violence of living in the modernizing world. Her perspective is valuable for putting into context the modernization and liberation narratives of the 1960s. In many ways, the 1960s present the continuation of a process begun in the 1920s and then put on hold by the calamities of the Second World War and post-war reconstruction. The dominant questions of the era were those of modernity itself: Would technology provide liberation from oppressive forms of labour? How would the modern world reconfigure traditional social relationships and hierarchies? What would state welfare provisions mean for the role of the family? As Hansen writes, '[cinema] was above all (at least until the rise of television) the single most expansive discursive horizon in which the effects of modernity were reflected, rejected or denied, transmuted or negotiated. It was both part and prominent symptom of the crisis as which modernity was perceived.'[20] According to Hansen's perspective, cinema in the fullest sense was a privileged site of experience, a way of achieving a temporary alienation of the everyday, something that the avant-garde was also working to achieve, but for a smaller, more select group.

Kracauer's theory of realism is refreshingly unconcerned with authenticity associated with lack of interference. Perhaps because of his connection to the German philosophical tradition of critique, he seems relatively unburdened by a positivist notion of visible evidence. As Geoffrey Nowell-Smith notes, the positivist view of truth, equating observable facts with truth, is counterbalanced by the post-Kantian philosophical tradition, 'which asserts that truth is not just there to be grasped but can only be elicited by a process of critique.'[21]

In this sense, imitation of life is not so much derivative as it is productive of a new insight into reality. According to this view, reality must be grasped actively through critique rather than merely passively through evidence. As has been pointed out by many a documentary film commentator, the same images can be made to signify in any number of ways. Images are contextualized through montage, but also through the act of filming itself, usually a purposive activity guided by conceptual frameworks.

Performance, with its theatrical trace, remains a troubled term in discussions of documentary film. From early experiments with form that tried to separate the cinematic from the theatrical (Eisenstein; Vertov) to observational cinema's unresolved contradictions about self-evidence, performance has often borne the brunt of the anxiety about depictions of reality. In many ways, it seems plausible to think about this anxiety as a product of the ideology of transparency where truth and fiction can be clearly signalled with different forms, their admixture carefully monitored, discussed, and regulated. A concept more challenging to twentieth-century ideas of 'film truth' has been posited by experimental and self-reflective forms of documentary filmmaking that have tended to foreground performance and mediation. As American non-fiction filmmaker Errol Morris has put it, there must be constant reminders that 'truth is not guaranteed' by film form.[22]

The strong reaction created by media texts deemed epistemologically troubling is culturally significant. In her famous study *Purity and Danger* (1966), anthropologist Mary Douglas highlighted the structures that lend meaning to human cultures. The cultural category of 'purity,' she found, shared an ambiguous relationship with that of 'danger.'[23] If we think of 'authenticity' or 'veracity' as the cultural category connected to 'purity,' its dangerous doppelgänger is 'performance.' Many times, the quest to determine the limits of performance and the existence of authenticity tends to overwhelm other kinds of discussions about media texts with claims to reality. This makes these texts into cultural barometers where, rather than discerning truth from fiction, we can read the anxieties of a positivist epistemology that longs for innocent images shorn of politics, interpretation, or conceptual work. *A Married Couple* interrupts those fantasies and, for that reason, remains a provocative text.

If it is possible to set aside naïvely technical notions of realism, reality-based work can be considered not solely in terms of form, but also in terms of intention and ethos. Unlike most forms of reality TV, Allan King's achievement in *A Married Couple* was to establish a relationship of trust with his film subjects and craft from observation of their lives as played for the camera, a meditation on intimacy and the family unit.

Where reality TV puts the observational camera into contrived situations, King based his film on an interconnection between filmmaker and film subject. His purpose was not to capture an unmediated picture of the Edwards's relationship, but rather to utilize mediation as a means to a higher level of insight for the filmmaker, the film subjects, and, potentially, audience members.

In order to achieve this new way of working with people in their own domestic space, King crafted a new film form, the 'actuality drama.' The experiments with both domesticity and form recorded in and expressed by the film, were of their moment and therefore unrepeatable. They traded in contemporary issues of therapeutic exploration and an avant-garde questioning of frames of perception. As in all of the most successful dramatic experiences, audience members are left with more questions than they started with. Like all the best observational cinema, *A Married Couple* asks the viewer to see beyond preconceptions. However, as a text that also challenges and questions our desire for raw reality while offering us a complex portrait of mediation, *A Married Couple* is an extremely rewarding film to think with. It certainly indicates that there are more categories to the docufictional than docudrama, mockumentary, and neo-realism.

Conclusion: The Legacy of
A Married Couple

In many ways a highly successful Canadian film, *A Married Couple* suffered rebuffs similar to those later experienced by *An American Family*. Jeffrey Ruoff points out that 'many critics failed to make distinctions between representation and reality' and that commentators were quick to locate the show within the despised 'therapeutic society thriving on "compulsion to confess."'[1] Jean Baudrillard discusses *An American Family* at length in *Simulations*. It is his privileged object of description, characterized as the 'the liturgical drama of a mass society.'[2] Because the American series was a combination of observational documentary and aspirational TV family familiar from situation comedies and soap operas, the series was denounced for its popular cultural debasements of a serious form. It was often discredited as being nothing more than a home movie.[3]

Although *A Married Couple* was not attacked on grounds associated with its form in the same way that *An American Family* was, its status as a feature film in a nation just finding its way in that area led to considerable scrutiny and just as much criticism. Was the private family life of a couple, perceived to be exhibitionist, appropriate content for a feature film? How had the process of making the film contaminated the possibility of a desirable Canadian cinema? What were the implications for films of the future: would Canada be awash in films starring the friends of filmmakers?

Ruoff asserts that *An American Family*'s 'greater merit lies in opening up the institution of the family, and issues of gender, sexuality, and interpersonal relations, to serious non-fiction film and video.' In the 1970s documentary film turned increasingly to intimate subject matter, and 'thanks to *An American Family*, interpersonal relations, family, gender, and sexuality have now become staples of American nonfiction film and video.'[4] Given that Gilbert and Ruoff acknowledge *An American Family*'s debt of inspiration to *A Married Couple*, what can we say about the legacy of *A Married Couple* for filmmaking in Canada and elsewhere?

A Married Couple is a landmark film that broke ground because of its highly original combination of documentary and drama as well as its boundary-transgressing depiction of the private sphere. Despite aspects of national embarrassment, the controversies raised by *A Married Couple* not only helped to put Canadian cinema on an international map, but also enacted an original combination of film ideas that fit well within a Canadian tradition of working with and against documentary. As a nation, Canada's dominant cinematic output until the 1960s was documentary produced at the National Film Board and the Canadian Broadcasting Corporation, an institutional reality reflected in King's own early career at the national broadcaster. Yet within that public service mandate, filmmakers were adept at stretching the boundaries of documentary, docudrama, and realism.[5] *A Married Couple* is a unique, perhaps unrepeatable combination of those elements. Like all feature-filmmaking in Canada at the time, it amazed commentators with its capacity to make local stories into theatrical successes. Coming out on the eve of the 1970s, just a couple of years after the formation of the Canadian Film Development Corporation, it seemed to provide a direction for Canadian cinema.

At the same time, its engagement with issues of domesticity and 'suburban enclosure' placed it squarely within the concerns of the day regarding the future of the nuclear family. As personal expectations shifted and issues of gender took centre stage, Allan King and his contemporaries were compelled to invent new modes of expression. A Married Couple is the inspired result of the confluence of social issues and experimentation in film form.

Allan King went on to make the controversial Come on Children (1973), which dealt with the dead ends of youth drug culture. Then, his experiment with documentary and therapeutic performance complete for the time being, he turned his hand to fiction, making a string of well-received feature films, such as Who Has Seen the Wind (1977), and directing episodic television shows, from Alfred Hitchcock Presents to Ready or Not, Danger Bay, and Road to Avonlea. His 1983 documentary about unemployment, Who's in Charge? caused a furore on the pages of Cinema Canada and elsewhere. Part of the premise of the film involved unemployed people being filmed while appearing on a stage for an arbitrarily limited amount of time (much like a counselling session). The film is a record of this social experiment and the subjects' frustrations and anxieties apparent in the end product provoked Michael Dorland to call King a sadist.[6] In his final decade, King returned to documentary, producing a series of affecting observational pieces about old age and death, Dying at Grace (2003) and Memory, For Max, Claire, Ida and Company (2005), and about racism, Emp4Life (2006). As these final films attest, a constant throughout his life's work was his non-judgmental, non-prejudicial vision. The relationships that King made with his documentary subjects were based on trust and respect, and that ethical stance is an enduring aspect of his work.

Throughout his long and distinguished career, King crafted a balance, perhaps unique in Canada, between experimentation and popular fare. He was certainly among the most prolific film artists this country has ever produced. The influence of A Married Couple is hard to measure. Its own concept was so daring, its experiment so historic, that with its realization came the end of a set of possibilities for documentary melodrama. On the other hand, the rise of mockumentary in Canada in the past couple of decades might be seen as a legacy of this and other direct cinema features of the 1960s and 1970s. Rather than emulate King's accomplishment, filmmakers working in the narrative film tradition in Canada might be said to have taken his lead in continuing to explore the zones of contact between fiction and documentary.

In *A Married Couple*, King showed what was possible in the context of a set of concerns about authenticity in both film and life that characterized the late 1960s. However, the interest in recent years in mockumentary and reality TV is not really a continuation of King's concerns and those of his contemporaries so much as a pale shadow of them. Where King sensitively probed the question of ethical engagement with real people acting in unscripted situations, rejecting any naïve technological guarantees, reality TV and mockumentary often fall into technologically determinist traps of mistaking the apparent immediacy of observational shooting with 'reality' itself. While reality TV is routinely scrutinized for the same elements as King's film was – performer motivation and authenticity – often these discussions are answered with simple binaries (real/fake) or fairly predictable observations about surveillance and the society of the spectacle.

King's film is the unique result of negotiating with undecidable issues around performance and reality, of accepting that one could start with questions and produce yet more questions. Not only did he answer to social scientific and aesthetic ideas of the day about the scripts embedded in institutions such as the family, he also crafted a memorable film experience not totally reducible to positivist questions of reality and fiction. Instead, King's film offers the viewer a vision of film as an 'imitation of life,' a form of mimesis that can offer us insight precisely because it is not a carbon copy of the visible world and would make no such claim. In its ability to heighten experience, through both participation in the filming experience and in the encounter with the finished film, *A Married Couple* gives us the nuanced insight of a filmmaker engaged with the complexities of film's vital encounter with reality. It seems to embody Kracauer's vision of the potentials of film for piecing together a fragmenting reality for fragmented beings. In his *Theory of Film*, originally published in 1960, Kracauer wrote:

> Film renders visible what we did not, or perhaps even could not, see before its advent. It effectively assists us in discovering the material world with its psychophysical correspondences. We literally redeem this world from its dormant state, its state of virtual nonexistence, by endeavouring to experience it through the camera. And we are free to experience it because we are fragmentized. The cinema can be defined as a medium particularly equipped to promote the redemption of physical reality. Its imagery permits us, for the first time, to take away with us the objects and occurrences that comprise the flow of material life.[7]

A Married Couple shows us daily life as it had never quite been seen before: incredible and terrifying in its ordinariness. In light of the social shifts and media forms that have emerged in the decades that followed, it is perhaps no exaggeration to say that we are all the children of *A Married Couple*.

Production Credits

Production Company

Aquarius Films

Director

Allan King

Cast

Antoinette Edwards
Billy Edwards
Bogart Edwards

Cinematographer and Associate Director

Richard Leiterman

Sound

Chris Wangler

Editor

Arla Saare

Music

Zaiman Yanovsky and Douglas Bush

Running Time

97 minutes

Aspect Ratio

1: 1.33

Further Viewing

An American Family. Craig Gilbert. 1973
Faces. John Cassavetes. 1967
Goin' Down the Road. Don Shebib. 1970
High School. Frederick Wiseman. 1968
Nobody Waved Goodbye. Don Owen. 1964
Scenes from a Marriage. Ingmar Bergman. 1973
Warrendale. Allan King. 1967

Notes

1. Introduction

1 Martin Malina, 'Unique Cinematic Experiment Hailed,' *Montreal Star*, 14 November 1969, 15.

2 Clyde Gilmour, 'Can a Husband and Wife Ever Forget the Camera?' *Toronto Telegram*, 7 November 1969, 50.

3 Les Wedman, 'A Married Couple is Coming to Town,' *Vancouver Sun*, 13 February 1970, 11A.

4 King filmed a Living Theatre production of *The Brig* in London in 1962 and later a production of Bertolt Brecht's play *Red Emma* (1976).

5 John Hofsess, *InnerViews: Ten Canadian Filmmakers* (Toronto: McGraw-Hill Ryerson, 1975), 65.

6 Ibid.

7 Sarah Polley, 'Allan King,' *Brick* 84 (Winter 2010), 38.

8 The NFB had produced realist features in the mid-1960s: *Le Chat dans le sac* (dir. Gilles Groulx, 1964) and *Nobody Waved Goodbye* (dir. Don Owen, 1964). In contrast to *A Married Couple*, these were fiction films made in the observational style.

9 Between *Warrendale* and *A Married Couple*, Wiseman worked with the King's long-time collaborator, cameraman Richard Leiterman, on *High School* (1968).

10 Rabinowitz, *They Must Be Represented*, 131–3.

11 Ruoff, *An American Family*, 12.

12 R.D. Laing, *The Politics of the Family* (Toronto: CBC, 1969), 1, 19–20.

13 Goffman, a Winnipegger trained at the University of Chicago, was a prominent public intellectual who contributed frequently to the CBC flagship show, *Ideas*. My thanks to Dylan Mulvin for this piece of Canadian radio history.

14 Samuel Weber, *Theatricality as Medium* (New York: Fordham University Press, 2004), 8.

15 Thomas Waugh, 'Acting to Play Oneself: Notes on Performance in Documentary,' in *Making Visible the Invisible: An Anthology of Original Essays on Film Acting*, ed. Carole Zucker (Metuchen, N.J.: Scarecrow, 1990), 64–91.

16 Paul Wilkins, *Psychodrama* (London: Sage, 1999), 12.

17 Alan Ackerman and Martin Puchner, 'Introduction: Modernism and Antitheatricality,' in *Against Theatre* ed. Ackerman and Puchner (Houndsmills: Palgrave Macmillan, 2006), 2.

18 Arnold Aronson, *American Avant-garde Theatre: A History* (London: Routledge, 2000), 48.

19 While cinéma-vérité emerged from a francophone tradition associated with the work of Jean Rouch, and to some degree Gilles Groulx and Michel Brault, direct cinema is associated with the work of American filmmakers such as Robert Drew, D.A. Pennebaker, and Albert and David Maysles. However, owing to the complexity of the films and traditions, rather than parse the terms further I choose to follow Bill Nichols in using the term 'observational cinema' to refer to both cinéma-vérité and direct cinema. As Nichols notes, observational cinema is a broader term for a style of filmmaking committed not only to on-the-spot filmmaking, but also to an ethos of attentiveness and ethical conduct towards film subjects. For a full discussion, see Bill Nichols, *Representing Reality: Issues and Concepts in Documentary* (Bloomington: Indiana University Press, 1991), 38–44.

20 Wintonick, Dir. *Cinéma Vérité: Defining the Moment*. Canada, 1999.

21 Chanan, *The Politics of Documentary* (London: BFI, 2007), 215.

22 Ibid., 224

23 Mark Andrejevic, *Reality TV: The Work of Being Watched* (New York: Rowan and Littlefield, 2004); Laurie Ouellette and James Hay, *Better Living Through Reality TV* (Oxford: Blackwell, 2008).

2. Observatonal Feature Filmmaking and the 'Dramaturgical Perspective'

1 For a list of Allan King's extensive filmography see www.allankingfilms.com.

2 Rosenthal, 'A Married Couple,' 23, 26.

3 Ibid., 50, 27–8.

4 Ibid., 47, 31.

5 Blaine Allen, Seth Feldman, and Peter Harcourt, 'Allan King Plus Three,' in *Allan King: Filmmaker* (Toronto: Toronto International Film Festival, 2002), 84.

6 Rosenthal, 'A Married Couple,' 25.

7 Ibid., 21 .

8 Feldman, 'Paradise and Its Discontents: An Introduction to Allan King,' in Feldman, *Allan King* , 4.

9 John Hofsess, *InnerViews: Ten Canadian Filmmakers* (Toronto: McGraw-Hill Ryerson, 1975), 64.

10 Martin, *Allan King*, 16.

11 Rosenthal, 'A Married Couple,' 32.

12 See Thomas W. Benson and Carolyn Anderson, *Reality Fictions: The Films of Frederick Wiseman*, 2nd ed. (Carbondale: Southern Illinois University Press, 2002).

13 See Brian Winston, *Claiming the Real* (London: BFI, 1995).

14 Ruoff, *An American Family*, 34.

15 Rosenthal, 'A Married Couple,' 64

16 Ibid., 29

17 Allen, Feldman, and Harcourt, 'Allan King Plus Three,' 83.

18 Frank Spotnitz, 'Frederick Wiseman: A Documentarist Who Sees His Work as Manipulation and Sport,' *American Film* 16 (May 1991), 18.

19 Rosenthal, 'A Married Couple,' 51.

20 Ibid., 46.

21 James E. Combs and Michael W. Mansfield, 'The Perspective of Life as Theatre,' in *Drama in Life: The Uses of Communication in Society*, ed. James E. Combs and Michael W. Mansfield (New York: Hastings House, 1976), xiv; Goffman, *The Presentation of Self in Everyday Life* (New York: Anchor Books, 1959), 72.

22 Goffman, *The Presentation of Self*, 106, 145.

23 Ibid., 112.

24 Chanan, *The Politics of Documentary* (London: BFI, 2007), 229–30, 226.

25 Paul Arthur, 'No Longer Absolute: Portraiture in Amercian Avant-Garde and Documentary Films of the Sixties,' in *Rites of Realism: Essays on Corporeal Cinema*, ed. Ivone Margulies (Durham, N.C.: Duke University Press, 2003), 99.

26 Žižek, *Looking Awry: An Introduction to Jacques Lacan Through Popular Culture* (Cambridge, Mass.: MIT Press, 1991).

27 Hilary Radner, 'Introduction,' in *Swinging Single: Representing Sexuality in the 1960s*, ed. Hilary Radner and Moya Luckett (Minneapolis: University of Minnesota Press, 1999), 30.

28 Rabinowitz, *They Must Be Represented*, 136.

29 Kozloff, *Overhearing Film Dialogue* (Berkeley: University of California Press, 2000), 14, 19.

30 Chanan, *The Politics of Documentary*, 218, 220.

31 Nichols, *Representing Reality: Issues and Concepts in Documentary* (Bloomington: Indiana University Press, 1991), 41–2.

32 Rosenthal, *A Married Couple*, 65.

3. *A Married Couple* as Documentary Melodrama

1 James Hay extends Raymond Williams's analysis of the intensification of regimes of mobility and privacy in the post-war family home. Hay, 'Unaided Virtues: The (Neo)Liberalization of the Domestic Sphere and the New Architecture of Community,' in *Foucault, Cultural Studies, and Governmentality*, ed. Jack Z. Bratich, Jeremy Packer, and Cameron McCarthy (Albany: State University of New York Press, 2003), 168–9.

2 Arthur, 'No Longer Absolute: Portraiture in Amercian Avant-Garde and Documentary Films of the Sixties,' in *Rites of Realism: Essays on Corporeal Cinema*, ed. Ivone Margulies (Durham, N.C.: Duke University Press, 2003), 100.

3 Thomas Frank, *The Conquest of Cool: Business Culture, Counterculture, and the Rise of Hip Consumerism* (Chicago: University of Chicago Press, 1997).

4 Ibid.

5 Email correspondence with author, 4 December 2008.

6 Rosenthal, 'A Married Couple,' 59.

7 Lea F. Frey, 'In diesen heil'gen Hallen,' www.aria-database.com/translations/mflute15_diesen.txt (Accessed 11 June 2009).

8 Rosenthal, 'A Married Couple,' 36.

9 Elsaesser, 'Tales of Sound and Fury: Observations on the Family Melodrama,' in Movies and Methods, Vol. 2, ed. Bill Nichols (Berkeley: University of California Press, 1985), 174.

10 Kozloff, Overhearing Film Dialogue (Berkeley: University of California Press, 2000), 239, 242.

11 'It has, of course, occurred to me in recent years – I've had plenty of time to ruminate over the course of my films, and my long silence since A Married Couple five years ago – that I expect too much from films, or from film audiences, and that this educative aspect which I would like to see as part of the film entertainment, rarely, if ever, works.' King, in John Hofsess, InnerViews:Ten Canadian Filmmakers (Toronto: McGraw-Hill Ryerson, 1975), 62–3.

12 Elsaesser, 'Tales of Sound and Fury,' 177.

13 Ibid., 182.

14 Vivian Sobchack, 'Lounge Time: Postwar Crises and the Chronotope of Film Noir,' in Refiguring American Film Genres: History and Theory ed. Nick Browne (Berkeley: University of California Press, 1998), 130, 148.

15 Elsaesser, 'Tales of Sound and Fury,' 182, 183.

16 Ibid., 170.

17 Daniel Boorstin, The Image: A Guide to Pseudo-events in America (New York: Atheneum, 1961).

4. Promotion and Reception

1 In some versions, a maple leaf is pasted across Bogart's genitals.

2 Blaik Kirby, 'Stars of Couple Found Film Showed Too Little,' Globe and Mail, 7 November 1969, 13.

3 Robertson, 'What People Are Doing,' Toronto Telegram, 2 January 1970, 39.

4 Mikos, 'Married Couple: Our Most Important Feature Film Yet,' Toronto Daily Star, 7 November 1969, 28.

5   Barnes, 'Theater: "Hair" Moves into Toronto,' *New York Times*, 13 January 1970.

6   'The Year's Best Films,' *Time*, 4 January 1971, 58.

7   Delany, 'A Married Couple.'

8   Eliscu, 'Thilm,' *East Village Other*, 14 January 1970, 21–2.

9   Gilmour, 'Clyde Gilmour's 10 Best and 50 Worst Movies of the Past Year … And More of the Same,' *Toronto Telegram*, 3 January 1970, C2.

10 Kael, 'The Current Cinema,' 114.

11 Canby, 'Screen: Elusive Reality,' *New York Times*, 3 February 1970, 38.

12 Haskell, 'Films: Three Documentaries,' *Village Voice*,29 January 1970, 53.

13 Marcorelles, 'La Quinzaine des Réalisateurs au Festival de Cannes,' *Le Monde*, 13 May 1970, 21.

14 Blumer, 'A Married Couple,' *Take One* 2 (March-April 1969), 22.

15 'Dissection of a Marriage,' *Time*, 26 January 1970, 79.

16 'A Married Couple,' *Maclean's*, January 1970, 79.

17 Delany, 'A Married Couple,' 65.

18 Roland Gelatt, 'SR Goes to the Movies,' *Saturday Review*, 24 January 1970, 47.

19 Strick, 'A Married Couple.'

20 Crist, 'Substance within the Square,' *New York*,26 January 1970, 55; Wedman, 'A Married Couple is Coming to Town,' *Vancouver Sun*, 13 February 1970, 11A.

21 Gilmour, 'Can a Husband and Wife Ever Forget the Camera?' *Toronto Telegram*, 7 November 1969, 50.

22 Joseph Morgenstern, 'Better Halves,' *Newsweek*, 2 February 1970, 83.

23 Aronoff, 'A Married Couple Emasculated,' Montreal *Gazette*, 15 November 1969, 14.

24 Knelman, '96 Tender, Tough, Touching Minutes,' *Globe and Mail*, 7 November 1969, 13.

25 Zolf, 'Films,' *Maclean's*, August 1969, 70.

26 Canby, 'Screen: American Dream,' *New York Times*, 23 April 1971, 17.

27 Crist, 'Substance within the Square,' 55.

28 Harris, 'Now the Warrendale Man Takes an Intimate Look at Marriage,' *Toronto Daily Star*, 7 December 1968, 65.

29 Wedman, 'A Married Couple is Coming to Town,' *Vancouver Sun*, 13 February 1970, 11A.

30 Malina, 'Unique Cinematic Experiment Hailed,' *Montreal Star* 14 November 1969, 15.

31 Sobchack, 'Toward a Phenomenology of Nonfictional Film Experience,' in *Collecting Visible Evidence*, ed. Jane Gaines and Michael Renov (Minneapolis: University of Minnesota Press, 1999), 249.

32 Ibid., 244.

33 Ibid., 251.

5. Imitation of Life? Towards a Theory of Documentary Mimesis

1 King, 'More Muddy Morals: A Reply to Critics,' *Cinema Canada* 104 (February 1984), 7.

2 Rhodes and Springer, 'Introduction,' in Rhodes and Springer, *Docufictions*, 4; italics in original.

3 Rabinowitz, *They Must Be Represented*, 130.

4 Rothman, *Documentary Film Classics*, 111.

5 Feldman, 'CBC Docudrama Since *The Tar Sands*: What's New?' *Cinema Canada* 142 (June 1987), 16.

6 See, for example, Feldman, 'CBC Docudrama'; Jeannette Sloniowski, 'Popularizing History: *The Valour and the Horror*,' in *Slippery Pastimes: Reading the Popular in Canadian Culture*, ed. Joan Nicks and Jeannette Sloniowski (Waterloo: Wilfrid Laurier University Press, 2002); Lyle Dick, 'Representing National History on Telelvision: The Case of *Canada: A People's History*,' in *Programming Reality: Perspectives on English-Canadian Television*,' ed. Zoë Druick and Aspa Kotsopoulos (Waterloo: Wilfrid Laurier Univerity Press, 2008).

7 Williams, *Television: Technology and Cultural Form* (London: Fontana, 1974), 72.

8 Paget, *No Other Way to Tell it: Dramadoc/Docudrama on Television* (Manchester: Manchester University Press, 1998), 3, 89.

9 Ibid., 61.

10 Jane Feuer, *Seeing Through the Eighties: Television and Reaganism* (Durham, N.C.: Duke University Press, 1995).

11 John Corner, *Television Form and Public Address* (London: Edward Arnold, 1995), 199.

12 Hogarth, *Documentary Television in Canada: From National Public Service to Global Marketplace* (Montreal and Kingston: McGill-Queen's University Press, 2002), 22, 29.

13 Hogarth, 'Reenacting Canada: The Nation-State as an Object of Desire in the Early Years of Canadian Broadcasting,' in Druick and Kotsopoulos, *Programming Reality*, 17.

14 Hogarth, *Documentary Television in Canada*, 62.

15 Paget, *No Other Way to Tell it*, 126, 137.

16 Thomas Waugh, 'Acting to Play Oneself: Notes on Performance in Documentary,' in *Making Visible the Invisible: An Anthology of Original Essays on Film Acting*, ed. Carole Zucher (Metuchen, N.J.: Scarecrow, 1999), 64.

17 Kracauer, *Theory of Film: The Redemption of Physical Reality* (Princeton, N.J.: Princeton University Press, 1997).

18 Hansen, 'Introduction,' in ibid., xxv, xxi, xxvii.

19 Kracauer, *Theory of Film*, 63, 99.

20 Hansen, 'America, Paris, the Alps: Kracauer (and Benjamin) on Cinema and Modernity,' in *Cinema and the Invention of Modern Life*, ed. Leo Charney and Vanessa R. Schwartz (Berkeley: University of California Press, 1995), 365.

21 Nowell-Smith, *Making Waves*, 89.

22 P. Bates, 'Truth Not Guaranteed: An Interview with Errol Morris,' *Cinéaste* 17 (1989): 16–17.

23 Douglas, *Purity and Danger: An Analysis of Concepts of Pollution and Taboo* (London: Routledge and Kegan Paul, 1966).

6. Conclusion: The Legacy of A Married Couple

1 Ruoff, *An American Family*, 105–6.

2 Baudrillard, 'The Precession of the Simulacra,' in *Art After Modernism: Rethinking Representation*, ed. B. Wallis (New York: New Museum of Contemporary Art), 271.

3 Ruoff, *An American Family*, v, 194.

4 Ibid., 136.

5 See Zoë Druick and Aspa Kotsopoulos, eds, *Programming Reality: Perspectives on English-Canadian Television* (Waterloo, Ont.: Wilfrid Laurier University Press, 2008).

6 Dorland, 'Pawns of Experience,' in *Cinema Canada* 102 (December 1983), 24.
7 Kracauer, *Theory of Film: The Redemption of Physical Reality* (Princeton, N.J.: Princeton University Press), 300.

Selected Bibliography

On Allan King

Feldman, Seth, ed. *Allan King: Filmmaker*. Toronto: Toronto International Film
    Festival and Bloomington: Indiana University Press, 2002.
Martin, Bruce. *Allan King: An Interview with Bruce Martin*. Ottawa: Canadian Film
    Institute, 1970.
Rosenthal, Alan. 'A *Married Couple*,' in *The New Documentary in Action: A Casebook in
    Film Making*, ed. Alan Rosenthal. Berkeley: University of California Press, 1971.

On Observational Documentary and Reality TV

Biressi, Anita, and Heather Nunn. *Reality TV: Realism and Revelation*. London:
    Wallflower, 2005.
Dovey, Jon. *Freakshow: First Person Media and Factual Television*. London: Pluto,
    1999.
Nowell-Smith, Geoffrey. *Making Waves: New Cinemas of the 1960s*. New York:
    Continuum, 2008.
Ouellette, Laurie, and James Hay. *Better Living Through Reality TV*. Oxford:
    Blackwell, 2008.
Rabinowicz, Paula. *They Must Be Represented: The Politics of Documentary*. London:
    Verso, 1994.
Rhodes, Gary, and John Parris Springer, eds. *Docufictions: Essays on the Intersection
    of Documentary and Fiction Filmmaking*. Jefferson, N.C.: McFarland, 2006.

Rothman, William. *Documentary Film Classics*. Cambridge University Press, 1997.
Ruoff, Jeffrey. *An American Family: A Televised Life*. Minneapolis: University of Minnesota Press, 2002.

Selected Film Reviews

Delany, Marshall. 'A Married Couple: New Departure for the Movies.' *Saturday Night* (November 1969): 65–6.
Kael, Pauline. 'The Current Cinema: Trends and Paroxysms.' *New Yorker* 45,52 (1970): 114–18.
Strick, Philip. 'A Married Couple,' *Sight and Sound* 39 (Autumn 1970): 219–20.

CANADIAN CINEMA

Edited by Bart Beaty and Will Straw